FASTING

Releasing the Miraculous
Through Prayer & Fasting

Dr. Maureen Anderson

Harrison House
Tulsa, OK

ISBN 13 1-978-1-60683-418-3

Fasting: Releasing the Miraculous Through Prayer & Fasting
Copyright © 2007 Winword Publishing
Phoenix, Arizona

Published by Harrison House Publishers
P.O. Box 35035
Tulsa, Oklahoma 74153
www.harrisonhouse.com

Contents

Dedication

*O*ver the years, I have been blessed by the support of many wonderful people who stood beside me to assist in the ministry of preaching and teaching the Word of God. It is always a team effort and I value every person who has committed themselves to being a part of my life in that way.

I dedicate this book to the loyal and hardworking team who have assisted so much in making this important teaching on fasting and prayer possible—David Crammer, Darlene Vinarskai, Shelley Johnson, Don Enevoldsen and Larry Walker. They have been an active part of every phase of production, from assistance with writing and cover design to proofing and getting the book printed and available.

I pray that God richly bless each of them for their dedication to the call of God in their lives.

1

The Baptist Ladies of Orfordville

*O*rfordville is a small town in Wisconsin, so small, that I don't think there was even a grocery store. That is where we lived after my husband, Tom, graduated from college. Tom was a teacher at the time, and he was hired to work in the local high school. Life there, as is often the case in small towns, revolved around the school.

Orfordville also had a small women's Bible study, started by four ladies from the local Baptist church. They always invited the teachers' wives and other women in the community to join them, but had experienced limited results. Some women came and occasionally they would go through the sinner's prayer, but then resume living as though they had never heard of Jesus.

These Baptist ladies wanted to make an impact on the women in their community, however, so they came up with a plan. Looking back, I have no doubt that the Holy Spirit inspired them. They decided to go on a fast. Specifically, they committed themselves to fasting and praying that one of the teachers' wives would get saved. They focused on a single salvation.

Since Tom was a teacher, that meant that I was included in their prayer. They didn't know me at the time, or anything about me. I had a completely different circle of friends and never saw them or talked to them. I didn't even know about their Bible study. I wasn't in their world at all. I don't think they had any idea what their fasting and prayer was about to do.

When those four little ladies started fasting and praying, however, my life was suddenly invaded by the supernatural. I woke up screaming at night. I had horrible dreams that I was going to die and go to hell.

I didn't know what to do. I was a very bad Catholic-I hardly ever went to church, maybe once or twice a year. Tom was Lutheran and he wasn't any more interested in church than me. Once in a while we would feel convicted and go, but not very often. I just knew that I was headed for hell.

I kept having bad dreams, night after night. All of a sudden, heaven and hell were incredibly real to me. Sin became real. Everywhere I went, I became aware of sin in my life and I lived in dread of the punishment for it. I felt like I was at a crossroad and I needed to make a decision, but I didn't know how to do it.

This went on all summer. The four Baptist ladies didn't know what I was going through. They couldn't know how much impact their fasting and prayer was having.

The school year finally started. I was asked to be one of the teachers' wives who helped plan an opening-day party for the teachers. I went to a planning meeting that included one of the Baptist ladies. In the course of the conversation, the Bible study was mentioned.

I was desperate. Right away I asked, "Can I come to your Bible study?"

The ladies looked at me a little surprised at how intensely I asked. "Of course, you can come. We want you to come." And they really did. I had never owned a Bible, and I suddenly realized that I needed one. They had one that they offered to give me.

On the way home, I rode with another friend of mine. She said, "Maureen, those ladies are nuts. You don't want to go to that Bible study. It's a nutty group."

Inside myself, though, I was so desperate that I didn't care. It didn't matter what my friend said. I was going. I could hardly wait. I worked as a nurse at the time and even at work, I said, "I'm going to a Bible study. I can hardly wait." The reactions from people indicated that they probably thought I was a little nutty myself.

Finally the day came. I got to the Bible study. They were waiting for me. My son, Jason, was a baby at the time. They put him in another room where someone would take care of him and the meeting started. Several women started giving their testimony about how they received Jesus and how wonderful their relationships with Him were.

I listened for a while and then I started to get mad. I had never had an experience with God. I thought, *What's wrong with me?* There was another woman there who had met Jesus in the

Catholic Church. I had been Catholic, so I had something in common with her. On my way out the door I told her, "I don't know what you are talking about. I've been a good person, and I've never had an experience with Jesus."

She said, "You need to pray the prayer." She then explained what the prayer was.

I thought, *Okay, the prayer, the prayer.*, hurried home and I couldn't wait. I had to get everybody to bed and then I would be alone and I could say the prayer.

At last, the moment came. Everyone was in bed. The day was over. I crawled into bed and said, "Okay, Father God." All of a sudden, I felt a conviction of sin.

I tried to roll over and I heard strong wind blowing outside. Wind is not unusual in Wisconsin in the fall, but I realized the window was open and that if a storm was coming, I needed to close it.

But then something happened that I wasn't expecting. Suddenly the wind was in the room. It was the presence of God and He just kept coming. He completely filled me. I was overwhelmed by it. Finally I said, "God, I can't take any more of You." He not only saved me, but I was baptized in the Holy Spirit at the same time. I had a genuine experience with God.

The next day, Tom woke up and he had a different wife. I had been transformed. He wasn't sure what had happened, but I was changed.

This was my first experience with the results of fasting and prayer. Those four ladies had no idea what their prayer was accomplishing, but my life was never the same after that.

Fasting and prayer brought me into the supernatural. If they had not decided to fast and pray, none of that would have happened.

Since that time, Tom and I have incorporated fasting into our lives on a regular basis. When we apply fasting, we see the supernatural and the miraculous. It is the Word of God that accomplishes the will of God, but fasting plays an important part in changing us, getting rid of any doubt or unbelief that keeps us from walking in faith and truly believing the Word.

Unfortunately, fasting has become an almost forgotten art in the church today. Occasionally a congregation will be asked to fast and pray about something, but rarely is any instruction given about how to fast. People are simply told to stop eating.

The process of fasting is so seldom taught that most Christians are very uneducated about the benefits, both spiritually and physically. It is those benefits that I want to explore in this book and then give some practical instruction about the right way to fast.

I believe that as you start to understand what fasting does, you will want to incorporate it into your own life. Before you do, however, I have to give one word of caution. Make sure that you learn how to do it the right way before you start. Fasting has a physical effect on you that you need to understand. If it is not done right, it can cause damage. For example, if you go on a fast for ten days and then sit down to a steak dinner, you will very likely put yourself in the hospital. Your stomach won't be ready for it.

Do not start fasting until you have read the entire book. You should also consult your doctor before going on a fast to make sure that there will be no complications because of a particular health issue, especially if you are diabetic, hypoglycemic, or if you have a heart condition or liver or kidney problems. (You might want to ask your doctor if he has any experience with fasting. Many don't.) If you are pregnant or a nursing mother, you definitely should not go on a fast. There are other considerations, as well. We will cover the dos and don'ts of fasting so that you can maximize the effects and not cause yourself physical problems. The last chapter gives some basic guidelines for what to eat and what not to eat.

Fasting is actually very good for you when you do it right. It will bring health to your body and it will bring your prayer life to a new level of effectiveness. It is something that we should all be doing. Notice that in Matthew 6:16, Jesus said, "When you fast," not, "If you fast." Fasting should be a regular part of our lives, for both physical and spiritual health.

With that in mind, let's examine just what fasting does, how it works and what the Bible has to say about it

Summary

1. Fasting and prayer bring the supernatural into your life. It is something we should do regularly. Jesus said, "When you fast," not, "If you fast."
2. Fasting needs to be done in the right way or it can be harmful.

3. Consult your doctor before going on a fast to make sure you won't have complications because of a health issue. Make sure your doctor has some experience with fasting.

4. You should not fast if:
   - you are diabetic,
   - you are hypoglycemic,
   - you have a heart problem,
   - you have liver problems,
   - you have kidney problems,
   - you are pregnant,
   - you are a nursing mother.

Application

1. You should not start fasting until you finish reading this book so that you will have the knowledge to do it right. You can, however, prepare yourself mentally and spiritually now. Most importantly, you can begin to fill yourself with the Word of God and with positive thoughts about fasting. At the end of each chapter, you will find Scripture Confessions that you should speak every day, as well as other suggestions and guidelines to prepare you for effective fasting and prayer.

2. For now, make sure that you do not have any physical condition that will hinder your fast. Consult your doctor. Make sure your doctor has some experience with fasting.

2

Cleansing the Body

*W*e should begin by defining just what it means to fast. The word "fasting," in both biblical Hebrew and Greek, means to go without food. In fact, the Hebrew word has the root meaning of "cover over," as in covering over your mouth. Fasting means to do without food. When we talk about it in spiritual terms, fasting is defined as a voluntary and deliberate abstinence from food for the purpose of concentrated prayer.

Fasting does not mean going without water. You can only go without water for about three days and even that is not good for you. You need to drink twice as much water during a fast as you normally would. It is the water that helps cleanse the toxins out of your body.

You should also drink juices during a fast. Make sure they are organic juices without any added sugar. At the end of this book, we will look at specifically what you should and shouldn't have while you are fasting. Organic fruit and vegetable juices will help keep your energy levels up so that you can go about your normal business while you are on a fast.

Before looking at the spiritual aspects of fasting, it is very important to understand what fasting does physically. We will find that the spiritual benefits are very similar to the physical benefits. To understand one is to understand the other. So we will begin by looking at the effects of fasting on our bodies.

First and foremost, fasting is a process of cleansing our cells from toxins. The reason that we need cleansing is because of the toxins that we accumulate in our bodies. Over time, toxins build up from a number of sources that cause diseases. They are absorbed through three basic means.

1. Eating

Our society has become so oriented toward fast food and convenience that we don't think about how many preservatives and other chemicals are used to keep the food from spoiling while it sits in the store. Other chemicals include perfumes and dyes that serve no purpose other than making the food look better so that you are more likely to buy it. Nearly everything we eat or drink adds to the buildup of toxins in our bodies. There are 14,000 food chemicals in modern American processed foods and medications. Just the basic overindulgence that is prevalent among Americans results in a high level of toxins.

2. Breathing

Every day we inhale a wide selection of toxins of which we are often not directly aware. Smoke and air pollution have become a standard part of American life. The air we breathe is filled with toxins that enter the body through the nose and lungs. Less obvious are things that are in our homes. Every day we inhale mold, dust, pollens, and fumes from things like carpets, new furniture, glue, paint and candles. Even air fresheners are full of toxins. Every time you take a breath, toxins enter your system.

3. Skin

Your skin is the largest organ in your body. Every time you use lotion, cosmetics, soap, shampoo or sunscreen, a certain amount of chemicals are absorbed directly into your body through your skin. All of those substances have toxins that become part of your body within minutes.

Elimination of Toxins

If we really knew how many toxins we take in each day, we would probably panic. Fortunately, the body is designed to eliminate them, but fasting has to be a part of the elimination so that disease doesn't take over the body. The body will constantly try to get rid of these toxins so that they don't adversely affect health, but it needs our help through fasting.

There are several ways that the body tries to rid itself of toxins. First, it will try to burn the toxins by converting them to energy. Secondly, the body will eliminate many toxins through the elimination process that is a natural part of digestion.

Those two methods will get rid of most of the toxins in your system, but not all of them. There are always some left over and the body deals with them by storing them in a safe place where they won't do any immediate harm. It hides them in your cells.

It is these left-over toxins that cause health problems for us if we leave them for too long. From time to time, the cells need to be cleaned out. Just like the closet or the garage where you put things you don't know what to do with, after a while, there is no more room, and some of the junk has to go. If the toxins are not cleaned out, they will eventually overwhelm your immune system and begin to affect your health. Your body needs fasting to do this house cleaning.

We experience high and low cycles. During the low cycle, the body expels toxins from the various cells where they have been stored and they are dumped into the blood stream. From there, they can be removed from the body. This low phase is a natural detoxification process. Fasting during this time aids the process and helps the body cleanse itself. By fasting, you help your body to clean house. You are allowing your body to take the energy that would normally be used in digesting food and focus it on cleaning cells.

It is during those down times that you experience the uncomfortable part of fasting. This can include a wide variety of symptoms that you might normally associate with something like the flu. During those down times, you might experience headaches, diarrhea, depression, nausea, weakness, fatigue, fever, muscle aches or bad breath. It is part of the cleansing process. It is not hunger that makes you feel bad when you are fasting. It is all of the toxins and poisons that are dumped into your system. The more toxins that you have built up, the worse you will feel. Fasting will speed the process, however, and help you get back to feeling good and having more energy.

Health Benefits of Fasting

This cleansing aspect of fasting is so important that fasting is actually a good way to bring healing from any disease. If you have ever had a pet dog or cat that got sick, you might have noticed that the first thing animals do when they are sick is stop eating. Digestion uses up a tremendous amount of energy. It takes several days for a single meal to work its way through your system, and all the time, your body has to use energy to digest, process and eliminate it.

When you stop eating, that energy can be redirected toward fighting disease and bringing healing. Your body is able to deal with the toxins in your system without the distraction of taking care of food that you have eaten. If you start fasting on a regular basis, your body will keep the toxins cleaned out before they cause other problems and healing will not be necessary. Fasting helps the body stay healthy. I have experienced miraculous healing when I have been sick so I know God can heal, but it is better to just stay healthy in the first place and not need the miracle.

Fasting also benefits your health by giving your body a rest. It can bring healing to a surprising variety of health problems. It might be more accurate to say that fasting rejuvenates your body more than it brings healing, but whatever you decide to call it, your health improves.

In the book *Prescription for Nutritional Healing,* James F. Balch, M.D and Phyllis A. Balch, C.N.C. describe some of the many and varied benefits from fasting. You heal faster, give your organs a rest, clean your liver and kidneys, purify your blood, cleanse your colon, lose unnecessary weight, get rid of toxin buildup in tissues, clear the eyes and tongue, cleanse the breath, and lose excess water. To realize these benefits, they recommend a three-day fast once a month and a ten-day fast twice a year. While fasting, your body will focus on cellular repair and rejuvenation. It will start with fat, tumors and damaged cells and then move on to rejuvenating vital muscle tissue and then work on restoring your essential organs.

There are so many health benefits that it is almost hard to believe, but all kinds of ailments will respond to fasting.

- Fasting helps the immune system to rebuild itself.
- Fasting fights off degenerative diseases.
- Fasting helps clear up allergies such as asthma, hay fever and bronchitis.
- Fasting helps improve rheumatism.
- Fasting can help eliminate insomnia.
- Fasting can get rid of migraine headaches.
- Fasting brings blood presure to healthy levels, whether you have high blood pressure or low blood pressure.

- Fasting improves arteriosclerosis.
- Fasting can clear up skin diseases such as acne, psoriasis, hives and boils.
- Fasting can help clear up ulcers.
- Fasting helps to eliminate liver problems.
- Fasting eliminates constipation.
- Fasting can eliminate gall stones.
- Fasting allows the body to self-digest and destroy needless tissue such as fat and tumors. While you are fasting, any abnormal growths in your body do not have the full support of the body's resources and they become more susceptible to being broken down to produce energy.
- Fasting can eliminate diarrhea.
- Fasting causes rapid, safe weight loss. In fact, you can't fast without losing weight. At the same time that the weight is dropping off, you will find your high blood pressure getting lower and the burden on your thyroid gland, endocrine system and adrenal glands reduced, along with the pressure on your heart.
- Fasting can break many food addictions, such as coffee or alcohol. In fact, a three-day fast will break any addiction, including smoking and other bad habits.
- Fasting can alleviate the effects of diabetes.
- Fasting eliminates plaque in the blood vessels.
- Fasting improves hypertension.

- Fasting reverses the aging process by causing a slower metabolic rate, more efficient protein production and an improved immune system. A study on mice verified this effect of fasting.
- Those who fasted every third day lived an average of forty percent longer than those who didn't.
- Fasting will clear your eyes, your tongue, and will cleanse your breath.
- Fasting lowers serum fats and thins the blood, which increases oxygenation and allows white blood cells to move more efficiently.

Fasting is extremely beneficial, but remember, you do need to fast in the right way. If you have a lifetime of accumulated toxins built up in you and then you suddenly dump them into your bloodstream, it is possible that you could experience toxic shock strong enough to kill you.

Don't panic, though, because there are ways to reduce the amount of toxins through a change in diet before you fast. Fasting isn't dangerous if you plan your fast and you do it right. But if you have a lot of toxins in your system because of years of unhealthy eating habits, you will very likely experience some uncomfortable side effects like headaches and diarrhea.

You will notice a few other unpleasant side effects as well. One of the ways that your body eliminates toxins is through your skin and through your mouth. You will probably notice that your breath smells bad and you might notice an increase in unpleasant body odor. That is not unusual. It just means that the body is getting cleaner. You may be tempted to use a lot of deodorant, but be careful. That will actually slow the process down. If your body has not been cleansed for a long time, it is possible that you will develop acne or blemishes on your skin. They will not last. It is just poisons being expelled from your system. Just keep in mind that it is better to go through a little discomfort while the toxins are coming out than to let them stay inside of you where they can cause all kinds of physical problems.

I don't want to alarm you with this information. Fasting really is healthy, but you need to know the risks. If you are highly toxic from years of eating the wrong kinds of food, you will need to ease yourself into a fast. You do that by changing your diet for a time before you fast and eating healthy foods that will start to reduce the toxins in your system slowly. Then when you do fast, your body is already partially cleaned out and there will not be nearly as many toxins dumped into your system. This is also one of the reasons for drinking a lot of water during a fast. Water helps to carry the toxins away as quickly as possible. At the end of this book, there are some guidelines that you can follow in order to do this so that your fast is safe and healthy.

Remember, too, that there is no danger of starving while you are on a fast. No matter how weak and hungry you feel, the truth is that most Americans would have to stop eating for about forty days before actual starvation sets in. It would take that long to use up the stored fat in their bodies.

Later in the book, I will give you the details about how to do a safe and healthy fast. For right now, the important thing to know is what fasting does for you. The single most important thing to remember about fasting is that it cleanses your body. When you fast, your body is able to get rid of toxins and purify itself. Fasting is for cleansing. Fasting is the only time an anti-aging hormone is released into your cells.

Summary

1. Fasting means to go without food.
2. In spiritual terms, it means a voluntary and deliberate abstinence from food for the purpose of concentrated prayer.
3. You need to drink plenty of water while fasting.
4. You should also drink fruit and vegetable juices. We have so many toxins in our food today that a pure water fast would put too much strain on the body.
5. Fasting is a cleansing process.
6. We accumulate toxins through what we eat, the air we breathe and the things we put on our skin.
7. The body eliminates most toxins either by turning them into energy and burning them or through the digestive system. The rest are stored in cells and need to be cleansed periodically or they cause health problems.
8. We experience regular high and low cycles. During the low cycles, the body tries to cleanse toxins out of the cells. Fasting aids this process.
9. It is not hunger that makes you feel bad when fasting. It is all the toxins being dumped into your system from the places where they have been stored

in your cells. This dumping of toxins may cause you to feel a variety of symptoms, including headaches, diarrhea, depression, nausea, weakness, fatigue, fever, muscle aches or bad breath.

10. Fasting will bring healing from all kinds of diseases. You aid the healing process by allowing your body to rest from the task of digestion and focus its entire energy on restoring your body and strengthening your immune system.

11. Fasting is the only time an anti-aging hormone is released into your cells.

Application

The following Confessions deal with the health benefits of fasting. Speak them out loud every morning before you start your day and every evening before you go to bed. If you have time during the day, confess them as often as possible.

I am keeping my body under control, making it subject to the Holy Spirit. (1 Corinthians 9:27)

During this fast, I am sanctifying, cleansing and detoxifying my body so I am fit for the Master's good work. (2 Timothy 2:20)

All my digestive organs are resting, and no toxins are being put into my body.

Fat and toxins are being broken down and expelled from my body.

My immune system is being strengthened through this fast. The aging process is being reversed in my body, and I am living a longer, healthier life.

My liver, kidneys and colon are being cleansed and my blood is being purified.

I am losing excess weight and water during this fast.

My breath and tongue are being cleansed.

My bones are being strengthened. (Isaiah 58)

3

Pure Faith

*N*ew believers usually have pure faith. They just met Jesus and there hasn't been enough time for doubt and unbelief to creep into their thinking. They can ask God for things and they just assume that He is going to answer them. No one has yet told them to think that sometimes they don't get what they ask for. In their innocence, they just ask God, expect it and they usually get it. They don't know any different at that point.

When my husband, Tom, first got saved, he had a bleeding ulcer that put him in the hospital. He came home, but they still had to run a variety of tests on his body to see where they needed to do surgery and determine what other treatment needed to be done.

On the way to get the tests done, Tom exercised the pure faith of a new believer. He said, "God, You have the power to heal me. If You want to, You could just heal me now."

That was it. That was all he prayed. And he was totally healed. He went in for the tests and they couldn't find anything wrong. That is the pure faith of a new believer at work.

This purity of faith is actually the primary spiritual reason for fasting. Over time, we go through many different experiences in life that cause doubt and unbelief to creep in and contaminate our faith. We lose the purity of our faith. Fasting with prayer is a means of cleansing ourselves of unbelief. In this respect, fasting does the same thing in a spiritual sense that it does for our physical bodies. It cleanses us.

By understanding the physical affects of fasting, we can better see what happens in the spiritual. In the physical, fasting cleanses us from toxins that are harmful to the body. In the spiritual, fasting cleanses us of the toxins of doubt and unbelief. It washes out the pollution that has gotten into our spirits.

Our faith is much like a car battery. At first, the battery works perfectly. The car starts up immediately when you turn the key. But then one day, it suddenly seems sluggish. Instead of the engine turning over right away, it drags a little. The battery seems to have difficulty starting the engine. You check the battery and it is at full power, but there is corrosion on the terminals. The corrosion keeps the power from flowing freely and the battery can't do what it normally does. Once the corrosion is cleaned off, the battery works fine.

In the same way, you can have great faith. You can be hearing the Word all the time, but the corrosion or pollution of doubt and unbelief can creep in and block the power of faith from flowing freely in your life. Fasting with prayer produces a spiritual cleanse that gets rid of the corrosion so that your faith can work effectively.

Fasting does not change God. It changes you. It makes your faith pure so that you can see mountains move in your life. The goal of fasting with prayer is not to get God to do something. It is to purify your faith so that you can connect to the promises of God without hindrance.

Faith is necessary. Without faith, it is impossible to please God (Hebrews 11:6). We have some understanding of faith and how it works. We know that faith comes by hearing and hearing the Word of God. We know that in life, we can have great faith because we are hearing the Word. That is why we love the Word. We embrace it.

But we still find that there are times when we don't experience the miraculous in our lives, not because we don't have great faith, but because there is pollution in our faith. Fasting with prayer won't bring you into great faith. That is a function of the Word. Fasting with prayer will bring you into pure faith.

The Kingdom of God runs by faith in the same way that your physical body is run by food. You are what you eat. We know that we need certain nutrients in our food. We eat fruits and vegetables and, even though we can't see the vitamins, minerals and other nutrients that are in the food, we know that we need them. So we eat the food we need. It is what our bodies need to be healthy.

The problem is that there are a lot of other things that get into our bodies along with the healthy food. There are chemicals and preservatives even in most of the good foods.

When we include all of the cookies and candy that we add to it, along with the other pollution that we experience every day, our cells begin to accumulate toxins, and these toxins will eventually detract from our health. To get rid of them, we have to go on a fast.

In the same way, we feed the Word of God into our souls because, even though we can't see exactly what happens inside of us, we know that the Word will build up our faith. My soul's prosperity is dependant on how much of the Word I get into me. So I embrace the Word, confess it and bind myself to it. I know that it will produce faith in me.

Just as there are pollutants in the food we eat, there are things that creep into our lives that bring doubt and unbelief. We have great faith because of the Word, but it has trouble working because of the unbelief that builds up as a result of circumstances, upsetting experiences we have had, things that other people have said or any number of negative influences that we experience. Even though we develop great faith, to be perfectly honest, we all have situations of doubt and unbelief. We say things that are not according to the Word of God, when the power of life and death is in our tongues. Situations occur. There is past junk in our lives. These are all spiritual toxins that get into our systems and prevent faith from working. Just as we fast to cleanse our physical bodies, we have to fast to get rid of the toxins of doubt and unbelief in our souls.

An incident occurred in the ministry of Jesus that gave Him the opportunity to teach His disciples the importance of purity in their faith. Jesus had taken three of His disciples, Peter, James and John, up on a mountaintop with Him. They experienced the exhilaration of seeing Jesus transfigured before them. It was an exciting mountaintop experience.

While they were gone, however, the other disciples found themselves a little over their heads with a situation they weren't prepared to handle. Jesus walked into the middle of it when He returned from the mountain. He found a crowd gathered around the disciples, embroiled in a loud dispute. He asked them what was happening.

Then one of the crowd answered and said, "Teacher, I brought You my son, who has a mute spirit. And wherever it seizes him, it throws him down; he foams at the mouth, gnashes his teeth, and becomes rigid. So I spoke to Your disciples, that they should cast it out, but they could not" (Mark 9: 17-18).

The disciples were just not up to handling that particular situation. They tried, but the demon wouldn't come out. Jesus immediately addressed the problem and told them why they couldn't do it.

He answered him and said, "0 faithless generation, how long shall I be with you? How long shall I bear with you? Bring him to Me" (Mark 9:19).

Jesus then cast the demon out and the boy was delivered. It is pretty clear from the English translation of this verse what Jesus thought was the reason for the disciples' failure, but it is even clearer in the original Greek. They were faithless. They were unbelieving and without faith. Literally, they were the same as a heathen or an infidel.

These were the same men who had been following Jesus around and watching all kinds of miracles. They had heard the Word. The problem was that their faith was polluted. There was corrosion on it.

In Matthew's account of the same incident, he tells us that later the disciples came to Jesus privately. Perhaps they thought that Jesus had been talking about someone else when He called them a faithless generation. They asked again why they had not been able to cast the demon out. Jesus repeated what He had said before and added more insight: "So Jesus said to them, Because of your unbelief; for assuredly, I say to you, if you have faith as a mustard seed, you will say to this mountain, Move from here to there, and it will move; and nothing will be impossible for you. However, this kind does not go out except by prayer and fasting" (Matthew 17:20-21).

Here again, Jesus used the word "unbelief," by which He implied that they were like heathens and infidels. They were unbelievers who had no faith. He then told them something about faith. If they had faith like a mustard seed, they would be able to speak to a mountain and it would move. With faith like a mustard seed, nothing would be impossible.

What is mustard-seed faith like? The aspect of mustard seeds that is most often talked about is their size. They are very small, meaning that it doesn't take a lot of faith to make big things happen. There is another characteristic, however, that you need to be aware of. It has to do with the purity of the faith.

A few chapters later, in Matthew 21:21, Jesus again used the idea of faith enabling you to move a mountain. There He added the statement that you must not doubt. It is not simply a matter of having a little faith. The quality of the faith matters, too. It has to be pure.

The mustard seed is not only small. It is also pure. It is the purest of seeds. While other plants can be combined with each other to form hybrids, the mustard seed cannot. You cannot mix it with another seed to make a better mustard plant. It is pure.

That is why Jesus chose the mustard seed to illustrate faith. It is the smallest of seeds and it is the purest of seeds. You don't have to have great faith to see the supernatural, but you do have to have pure faith. You have to get rid of the doubt and unbelief. You have to get rid of the pollution.

That's what happens to our faith. All of the garbage gets in, all the doubt and unbelief, and it prevents faith from working. But Jesus gave the solution. "This kind does not go out except by prayer and fasting."

It wasn't the demon that Jesus was talking about. It was the unbelief. The unbelief could only come out by prayer and fasting. Fasting is a cleanse. It cleanses your physical body and it cleanses your spirit. It gets rid of the corrosion that keeps your faith from working effectively. If your faith does not seem to be working, try fasting and get the doubt and unbelief out.

Summary

1. Fasting has the same benefits spiritually as it does physically. It cleanses.

2. Fasting and prayer result in pure faith. They cleanse you of the toxins of doubt and unbelief.
3. Fasting with prayer does not change God. It changes you. It purifies your faith so that you can connect to the promises of God without hindrance.
4. Without faith, we cannot please God (Hebrews 11:6). Faith comes from hearing the Word.
5. If our faith is polluted by doubt and unbelief, it becomes difficult for us to connect to the Word.
6. Doubt and unbelief can result from circumstances, from negative experiences we have had, from things other people say to us, or from past junk in our lives.
7. Jesus pointed out the problem through an incident with a demon that the disciples couldn't cast out of a young boy.
   a. He said that the disciples failed to cast out the demon because of their lack of faith, their unbelief. Their faith was polluted, impure.
   b. Jesus compared effective faith to a mustard seed. The significant factor was the purity of the seed. The mustard seed is pure. It cannot be mixed with other seeds. Mustard-seed faith is pure faith.
8. The quality of faith matters. It has to be pure.

Application

1. As you prepare for your fast, you will want to write down those areas for which you are fasting. Over the next few chapters, we will explore some of the areas

that might keep you from having pure faith. Begin now to consider what things need to change in your life. Answer the following questions:

   a. Are there circumstances that make it difficult for you to believe God?

   b. Are there things in your past or in your family that you believe hold you back?

2. Begin a journal in which you can empty your heart of the things that need changing in your life or that aren't right. With each chapter, we will add to the list as you see the areas where fasting and prayer will help you. To begin with, list the negative influences that hinder your faith. Hold them up to God. Confess them as the sin of unbelief and receive forgiveness.

3. Continue the Confessions of Health Benefits from the last chapter, but add the following Confessions to them:

I wholly commit this fast to You, Lord, presenting my body to You as a living sacrifice, holy, pleasing and acceptable to You. (Romans 12:1)

Fasting with prayer is a vital part of my Christian life.

I am humbling myself through this fast. (Hebrews 12:1)

I am not gratifying the desires of the sinful nature. My flesh is under control.

I am seeing things in their proper perspective through this fast.

I am being cleansed from doubt and unbelief, and I have entered into mustard-seed faith.

Desires that are not of God are being resurrected back to what God wants for me physically and spiritually.

4

The Next Level–
Fasting for Direction

When we got married, my husband, Tom, and I had quite a bit of baggage that we had to work through. Situations came up that we had to deal with, and often, we were stuck. Many times, we just didn't know what to do.

Tom was always very strong when it came to fasting with prayer, however. Fasting with prayer has been a huge part of our lives from the time we got saved. If Tom got stuck and didn't know what to do, or if he wasn't hearing God or seeing the results that he needed to see, he would say to me, "We're going on a three-day fast. We're going to fast and pray because we need a breakthrough. We need something to happen."

And then we would go on a three-day fast. During that fast, God would show us what the problem was. One of us might have needed to get free from something. There might have been some situation that went back to our forefathers that we needed to confront. Whatever it was, while we were on a fast, God showed it to us and we dealt with it.

We fasted with prayer over our family. When our children reached the age when they started dating, we knew that who they married was a very important part of reaching their destinies. We often went away for three days to fast and pray for them to find the right mate.

Fasting with prayer became a natural part of our lives. There was a point when Tom was a youth pastor, and we seemed to be stuck there. We felt that we needed to go to the next level, but we just couldn't seem to make any progress. We didn't know what the problem was, but every time that destiny seemed to come to us, it was snatched away.

God gave Tom a dream that he should go on a fast, so he did. We didn't know exactly why, but we did it in obedience. During that fast, God performed miracles in Tom's life, and he was then able to step into the next part of his calling in life and fulfill his destiny.

There were many things in the unseen world that we didn't know were there, but they held us back. There were circumstances that would not change without the supernatural. Fasting with prayer enabled us to move into what God wanted for us by revealing what we needed to deal with. As a result, we have been able to have what God said we should have in our marriage. Our children are what God said our family should be. Our church is what God said our church should be. When we needed to see circumstances change, we went on a fast with prayer and the miracles would happen.

The Bible speaks frequently of fasting and prayer. We have often overlooked it, but the great men and women of God always fasted. By looking at their lives, we can see what fasting with prayer is able to accomplish. Before we begin fasting, I want to look closely at many of the great men and women of God in the Bible who fasted and see what the benefits were to them. Many are familiar stories, but we have often missed the fact that they fasted and prayed. We have become so focused on the miracles that followed, we have ignored how the miracles came in the first place.

Paul and Barnabas are a good example of how important fasting with prayer was in the life of the early church. Both men had an apostolic calling. They had gone to Antioch and had seen the grace of God at work, so they began to build the foundation of the church in that city.

This was a time when they needed some direction. They were certainly moving into new territory that no one else had experienced. There were Gentiles starting to get saved and the potential that lay before them was staggering. They had the opportunity to spread the Gospel all over the civilized world. The question was how they should do it. They didn't know what the next step should be.

We have all experienced times when we hit a plateau in our lives and we just couldn't seem to get to the next level. We don't really know which way to go. But there is something stirring inside of us. I believe that Paul and Barnabas both had that stirring in them. They needed direction, so they went on a fast. In fact, all the spiritual leaders of the church in Antioch fasted with them. "As they ministered to the Lord and fasted, the Holy

Spirit said, Now separate to Me Barnabas and Saul for the work to which I have called them" (Acts 13:2).

There are several things that we should note in this verse. First of all, they fasted while they "ministered to the Lord." The Greek word translated "ministered" is *leitourgeo*. It means to be a public servant, to do acts of service, to function within the church in a public service of love. It means to work, to toil, as an effort or an occupation, to implement an act, a deed, doing labor or work.

What were they doing while they fasted and prayed? They were working. They were doing the same thing that they did other days. I've had people say, "How can I fast and pray? I have to go to work." Well, go to work while you are fasting. It is acceptable to God. Jesus said that when you fast, you should avoid calling attention to the fact that you are fasting: "Moreover, when you fast, do not be like the hypocrites, with a sad countenance. For they disfigure their faces that they may appear to men to be fasting. Assuredly, I say to you, they have their reward. But you, when you fast, anoint your head and wash your face, so that you do not appear to men to be fasting, but to your Father who is in the secret place; and your Father who sees in secret will reward you openly" (Matthew 6:16-18).

Clean yourself up and go about the day giving love. Fasting and prayer should be connected to ministering to others and to the Lord. Paul and Barnabas had plenty to do. They were building a church, after all. They did not let fasting take them away from those responsibilities. They continued to minister while they were fasting. They gave love and they worshiped God.

The second thing to notice is that the Holy Spirit spoke. In a fast, God will speak to you. When you need direction, when you need to hear from God, when you've hit a plateau and you feel stuck, fasting with prayer is a good way to clear out the distractions that make it difficult for you to hear from God. No matter what it is that you need, the problem is not that God isn't talking to you. It is just that you are not hearing Him.

Fasting with prayer opens the channels of communication and enables you to hear God clearly. When you fast, God will speak to you.

The Holy Spirit spoke to the leaders in Antioch and gave them direction. They were to separate Paul and Barnabas for the work that God had called them to. Through fasting and prayer, they were able to go to the next level that God had for them. They had built one church. They had established the foundation. Now God wanted to use them to build many churches.

This tells us that increase came through fasting with prayer. Not only did the church increase, but supernatural increase came into Paul's own ministry. The fast and prayer helped propel him into his God-given destiny. Ultimately, he built churches all over the known world. He wrote two thirds of the New Testament. Through fasting, he was able to let go of what he was doing and start on the course that God had set for him. The church at Antioch was his home church. That is the place to which he always returned. But God had other things for him to do. At that point, he was released and sent out.

In your life, from time to time you will hit a plateau. You want to go to the next level, but you don't know how to get there. You're not seeing the success that the Word of God says you should have. You don't know what to do next to get out of the rut that you're in. You need to fast so that you can get rid of the corrosion on your faith. You need to purify your faith so that you can hear the voice of the Holy Spirit and go to the next level that God has for you.

Paul and Barnabas understood the importance of fasting with prayer. They continued in their service to God and to others while they fasted. During the fast, they heard the voice of the Holy Spirit and they were launched to the next level in their destinies.

The same will happen for you. God wants to speak to you. It is the doubt and unbelief that keep you from hearing Him. Fasting and prayer will cleanse you of the corrosion and bring you to a place of hearing God with pure and uncontaminated faith.

The first reason for fasting is for direction.

Summary

1. One of the primary purposes of fasting and prayer is for direction.

2. Paul and Barnabas received the direction of the Holy Spirit to begin their first missionary journey as a result of fasting and prayer. Several aspects of effective fasting and prayer are demonstrated by their experience:

a. They fasted while they ministered. They continued working. Fasting is not a reason to shirk responsibilities.

b. Fasting should be connected to ministry to others.

c. The Holy Spirit spoke as they fasted and prayed. Fasting will clear distractions so that you can hear God clearly.

d. They moved to another level in their ministry. Increase comes from fasting and prayer.

Application

1. It may be that you are fasting and praying for direction. If so, write down in your journal exactly what it is that you need God to tell you. As you fast and pray, expect to receive a word from God that will give you direction and clarity in your life.

2. Continue to speak the Confessions every day. Add the following:

I am hearing clearly from God. (Acts 13)

My faith is purified. (Acts 13)

5

In the Lion's Den

*D*aniel is one of the most inspiring men of God in the Bible. He had every reason to feel sorry for himself, yet he became one of the most powerful men of faith who ever lived.

Daniel was taken to Babylon as a captive very early in his life. He was chosen as part of a small group of the captives to be trained for service in the Babylonian government. After he finished the training, he was placed in the king's palace where his considerable talent and his dedication to excellence brought him promotion to the highest position in the land next to the king. The king at the time, Darius, divided the entire Babylonian empire into 120 provinces called satraps. He divided those into three groups and put a governor over each one. Daniel was one of those three governors. Then the king considered raising him even higher: "Then this Daniel distinguished himself above the governors and satraps, because an excellent spirit was in him; and the king gave thought to setting him over the whole realm" (Daniel 6:3).

As with so many other great men of faith in the Bible, Daniel incorporated fasting into his life on a regular basis. In Daniel 9, he described a vision that he couldn't understand. In his desire to know the meaning, he began a fast that lasted for twenty-one days. He did not hesitate to include fasting in his prayer life just for the understanding that it brought him.

We know, then, that fasting with prayer was a significant part of Daniel's personal life. But it is interesting that on at least one occasion, he benefited from someone else fasting for him.

Daniel's incredible success didn't please everyone. There were many who were jealous of him and who wanted him to fail. He was a foreigner and it bothered many native Babylonians that he would be promoted over them. "So the governors and satraps sought to find some charge against Daniel concerning the kingdom; but they could find no charge or fault, because he was faithful; nor was there any error or fault found in him" (Daniel 6:4).

Such jealousy is common. We have probably all experienced it to some degree. I remember that when I was in high school, I was voted in as a cheerleader. I was the only junior voted onto the A-Squad. Not only that, they told me that I had received the highest scores that anyone had ever received in the school. That meant that I was made the captain of the cheerleading squad. Since all the other girls were seniors, that didn't go over very well. It was a rough year. No one wanted to do anything I suggested.

God can easily give us favor and blessing and promotion, but that doesn't mean that everyone around us will be thrilled. That was what happened in Daniel's life. His enemies looked for a way to discredit him, but his work was too good.

At last, however, they devised a plan. They knew that Daniel prayed three times every day. They also knew that he was so devout that he would not change that practice, no matter what. They thought that they would never find any way to discredit Daniel unless it was in relation to his faith, since that was the one area that he would absolutely never allow to be compromised.

They came in to the king and began to flatter him, telling him how great he was. Then they said that they were all agreed that he should be honored throughout the kingdom. They had written up a law that declared that no one would be allowed to pray to or petition any god other than Darius himself for thirty days. Anyone caught praying to some other god during that time would be thrown into a den of lions. They only needed the king to sign the law into effect.

The king was so flattered by the declaration that he signed it, and the law went into effect. The king did not even think about Daniel and the fact that he would ignore the law and continue to pray to God. The tradition of that kingdom was that once a law was signed, it could not be changed, even by the king himself. The trap was set. Even when Darius discovered the danger that Daniel was in, he could do nothing to stop it. All they had to do was wait for Daniel to pray, and they would be rid of him.

Naturally, even after Daniel was informed of the law, he continued to pray three times every day. His enemies approached the king and asked why Daniel was not being punished for his disobedience.

The king then realized what had happened. He did not want to lose Daniel. He saw that Daniel was a tremendous asset to the kingdom and to him personally. The Bible tells us that he tried everything he could to avoid having to do anything to Daniel: "And the king, when he heard these words, was greatly displeased with himself, and set his heart on Daniel to deliver him; and he labored till the going down of the sun to deliver him" (Daniel 6:14).

But it was to no avail. The law could not be changed. It was an impossible situation. The king understood, however, that when a situation is impossible and you can't figure out any way in the natural to solve it, then it is time to go on a fast. He had Daniel brought to him and made his own confession of faith, "Your God, whom you serve continually, He will deliver you." (Daniel 6: 16).

In other words, the king declared that there was no way that he could save Daniel. The lions were hungry and they would certainly kill Daniel if something supernatural didn't intervene. But he knew that Daniel was a praying man and that he fasted regularly and that God could certainly rescue him. The king didn't just rely on Daniel's faith, however. He then spent the night fasting and praying himself. "Now the king went to his palace and spent the night fasting; and no musicians were brought before him. Also his sleep went from him" (Daniel 6: 18).

It was an Old Testament practice to begin a short fast with prayer at three o'clock in the afternoon and fast until six o'clock the next morning. That is the reason the first meal of the day is called breakfast. They were breaking the fast. That is essentially what the king did. He was up all night praying. And his fasting with prayer brought the supernatural. In the morning, he rushed out to the place where Daniel had been confined all night with hungry lions.

"And when he came to the den, he cried out with a lamenting voice to Daniel. The king spoke, saying to Daniel, Daniel, servant of the living God, has your God, whom you serve continually, been able to deliver you from the lions?

"Then Daniel said to the king, 0 king, live forever! My God sent His angel and shut the lions mouths, so that they have not hurt me, because I was found innocent before Him; and also, 0 king, I have done no wrong before you" (Daniel 6:20-22).

You could almost say that because King Darius fasted and prayed, angels came and forced the lions to fast as well. Their fast ended after Daniel was removed from the den. In the next few verses, we find that not only was Daniel spared, but the king brought the men who had accused Daniel and had them and their entire families thrown into the den of lions where they were all killed. Fasting not only brought deliverance to Daniel, but it got rid of his enemies. Fasting with prayer brings the supernatural. In this case, it brought angels.

With Paul and Barnabas, we saw that fasting brought direction. In the life of Daniel, it brought understanding and revelation. Then it brought supernatural protection.

Summary

1. Daniel incorporated fasting with prayer into his life on a regular basis. Whenever he faced a crisis or any time he found something he couldn't understand, he fasted and prayed.
2. Daniel also benefited from the fast of someone else. Daniel's enemies set a trap that forced King Darius to throw Daniel into a den of lions. Darius spent the night fasting and praying. In the morning, he found that Daniel had been delivered. The fasting and prayer had brought in the supernatural, in this case, an angel that shut the mouths of the lions.
3. Fasting and praying is the best way to deal with an impossible situation. It brings the supernatural and it results in deliverance.

Application

1. If you are fasting because you are facing a crisis and you need supernatural deliverance, write in your journal exactly what you want from God. Read it out loud and then expect God to purify your faith through fasting with prayer to bring deliverance to you. Receive the deliverance now.

2. Add the following to your daily Confessions. (Note that all the Confessions are listed in the back of the book for easy reference.)

My faith and fasting bring supernatural increase and move mountains. (Acts 13)

God is rewarding me openly through this fast. (Matthew 5:16-18)

I am fasting as God has chosen. Bonds of wickedness are loosed off my life. I am completely free from oppression. Every yoke of bondage is broken off my life. Every heavy burden is lifted off of me through this fast. My light is breaking forth! My healing is springing forth speedily! My righteousness goes before me for I am established in righteousness. The glory of the Lord is my rear guard. When I call, the Lord hears and answers me. Through this fast, God is causing me to ride on the high places. (Isaiah 58:6-14)

6

Salvation to the Gentiles

*A*ngels are, by definition, messengers. We often see them in the Bible proclaiming something from God to various people. As with Daniel, they are frequently connected to fasting with prayer. A good example of that connection is the story of Cornelius.

Cornelius was what the Jews called a God fearer. Because he was a Gentile, the Jews didn't believe that he could ever attain the same degree of salvation that the Jews did. Gentiles could convert to Judaism, and many did, but they were still considered outsiders, and Jews were not allowed to associate with them. A faithful and righteous Jew was not even allowed to go into a Gentile's house.

The early Christians were all Jews, and they continued the Jewish prejudice against Gentiles. They did not believe that salvation was for anyone but the Jews. They still believed that it was wrong for any Jew to set foot inside the house of a Gentile, whether he was a God-fearer or not.

God had other ideas, however. A devout man named Simeon, who saw Jesus in the Temple shortly after He was born, prophesied this about Him:

"For my eyes have seen Your salvation

Which You have prepared before the face of all peoples,

A light to bring revelation to the Gentiles,

And the glory of Your people Israel" (Luke 2:30-32).

He was quoting a prophecy from Isaiah 42:6 that foretold that the Messiah would bring salvation to the Gentiles, not just the Jews. The problem was that this idea of Jews not interacting with Gentiles was so strong in the early church that no one would even consider the possibility that Gentiles could be saved.

Cornelius is described in Acts 10 as a man who was very devout and who feared God. He gave alms very generously. He was a Roman centurion in the Italian Regiment. He continually prayed. As a part of that prayer, he later told Peter that he fasted (Acts 10:30). We can see that Cornelius wanted to know God's will in his life and in his family more than anything else.

God did not disappoint him. Cornelius' fasting and prayer opened the door to the supernatural. It was God's will that the Gentiles be saved, so there needed to be a first Gentile Salvation so that everyone would know. God responded to the prayers and fasting of Cornelius by sending an apostle to him.

As Cornelius fasted and prayed, an angel appeared to him in a vision.

> "About the ninth hour of the day he saw clearly in a vision an angel of God coming in and saying to him, 'Cornelius!' And when he observed him, he was afraid, and said, 'What is it, Lord?' So he said to him, 'Your prayers and your alms have come up for a memorial before God. Now send men to Joppa, and send for Simon whose surname is Peter. He is lodging with Simon, a tanner, whose house is by the sea. He will tell you what you must do'" (Acts 10:3-6).

As with King Darius, fasting with prayer caused the supernatural to come and resulted in the visitation of an angel. Cornelius immediately obeyed the vision and sent servants to Joppa to find Peter.

But that wasn't the only supernatural thing to happen. If the servants had simply gone to Peter and asked him to come with them to the home of Cornelius, Peter, being a practicing Jew, would have told them that he could not enter the house of a Gentile. He mentioned this custom specifically when he later met Cornelius, "Then he said to them, 'You know how unlawful it is for a Jewish man to keep company with or go to one of another nation'" (Acts 10:28).

Peter would have told them he couldn't go and that would have been the end of it. But as Cornelius was praying and fasting, God sent a vision to Peter as well. Peter was resting on the roof of the house where he was staying when he suddenly fell into a trance.

"And saw heaven opened and an object like a great sheet bound at the four corners, descending to him and let down to the earth. In it were all kinds of four-footed animals of the earth, wild beasts, creeping things, and birds of the air. And a voice came to him, 'Rise, Peter; kill and eat.' But Peter said, 'Not so, Lord! For I have never eaten anything common or unclean.' And a voice spoke to him again the second time, 'What God has cleansed you must not call common'" (Acts 10:11-15).

This scene was repeated two more times and then the vision disappeared. While Peter was sitting and contemplating what this could possibly mean, the servants arrived from Cornelius. Because of the vision, Peter didn't even question it when the Holy Spirit told him to go with the men. The vision had prepared him. The prejudice that Peter had against Gentiles was supernaturally eliminated.

When Peter arrived, Cornelius was ready for him. He had called together all of his family and close friends and they were sitting and waiting for Peter to come and speak the good news of salvation to them. As Peter did so, the Holy Spirit fell on the crowd and they were baptized in the Holy Spirit, confirming that it was God's will for Gentiles to be saved.

It is not too much to say that because one man fasted and prayed, history changed. The Word of God was fulfilled. Salvation came as a light to the Gentiles. Fasting with prayer purified Cornelius' faith and brought in the supernatural. As with Daniel, it brought angels. It also overcame racial prejudice.

It is easy to forget how important the supernatural is in everything we do. This is the most important lesson to learn from the story of Cornelius. Fasting with prayer brought the supernatural and it invaded the life of Cornelius, his family and Peter. Even in normal circumstances, the Bible tells us in John 6:44 that no one can come to God unless the Father first draws him. In other words, it is impossible to be saved without the supernatural working.

In the case of Cornelius, it was not a normal situation. The Jewish customs that prohibited a Jew to enter the home of a Gentile made it absolutely impossible for Peter, or any other Jew for that matter, to ever present the Gospel to Cornelius. It took the supernatural intervention of the Holy Spirit to remove the obstacles to salvation for Cornelius and his family.

It was the supernatural that drew Cornelius and it was the supernatural that opened the door for him to receive. My own salvation story is a great example of how important this is. The ladies who fasted and prayed for the teachers at their local school had been praying and witnessing for a long time. They talked to people, invited them to a Bible study and prayed for them to get saved. But after years of effort, they had accomplished very little.

The day they started fasting with prayer, however, everything changed. Without even knowing what the results of their prayer and fasting were, they unleashed the supernatural into my life in a way that I could not ignore. The conviction of the Holy Spirit literally invaded my life and would not go away. I became painfully aware of my sin and how much I needed and wanted God. Every step of the way, I experienced the super-natural presence of God and it changed my life completely. It overcame every possible obstacle and God spoke to me directly.

I saw the supernatural in my life even before I was saved, and it has never stopped. No matter what it is that I need, if I find that I can't break through and get it, I immediately start fasting and praying. My faith is purified and, in response to pure faith, the supernatural comes.

Summary

1. Cornelius was a Gentile, and Jews were not allowed to associate with Gentiles. He wanted to serve God, however, and he fasted in order to find the will of God. His fasting and prayer overcame the well-established prejudice against Gentiles.
2. Fasting purified Cornelius' faith.
3. Fasting and prayer brought the supernatural to both Cornelius and Peter. Both received clear direction, and it brought salvation to Cornelius and his family.
4. Fasting and prayer also opened the door to preaching the Gospel to all Gentiles all over the world.
5. Fasting and prayer overcomes prejudice.

Application

1. If you are facing prejudice of some kind, whether it be racial, from your in-laws, at work or whatever, turn the situation over to God and expect Him to

bring you favor. Write in your journal what prejudice you face. Receive favor now.

2. Continue your daily Confessions. Add the following:

I am abounding with the favor of You, Lord, and I am full of Your blessings. (Deuteronomy 33:23)

I win favor with everyone who sees me. (Esther 2: 15)

7

In the Midst of the Storm

The Apostle Paul was perhaps the most influential man in the history of the Church, other than Jesus himself. We find him moving powerfully in every area of ministry wherever he went. There is one incident in his life in particular that demonstrated the effects of fasting with prayer.

Paul had gone to Jerusalem and was nearly killed during a riot when some of the Jews in the Temple thought he had brought a Gentile into the inner courtyard. He was rescued from the crowd by Roman soldiers and ended up under arrest for the next two years in Caesarea. At a critical moment in his subsequent trial, he appealed to Caesar. Since Paul was a Roman citizen, the law required that his case be heard by Caesar and that meant that Paul had to be sent to Rome.

The journey by ship proved to be very eventful. Paul was put with a number of other prisoners on board a ship that sailed first along the coast, then out to sea in contrary winds and past the island of Cyprus. They made several stops along the way, but at the city of Lycia, they changed to an Alexandrian ship that was sailing for Italy.

From there, they continued westward past Cnidus and along the coast of Crete, still sailing with difficulty because of the wind. They finally put in at a place called Fair Havens, where they apparently stayed for a while.

There are certain times of year in the Mediterranean when it is more dangerous to sail because of the likelihood of storms. Most ships would not even consider putting to sea during those times. It was late in the season and that time was approaching. Paul was the one who first suggested that they shouldn't go any further until after the storm season had passed: "Now when much time had been spent, and sailing was now dangerous because the Fast was already over, Paul advised them, saying, Men, I perceive that this voyage will end with disaster and much loss, not only of the cargo and ship, but also our lives" (Acts 27:9-10).

Paul felt a check in his spirit. The problem was that he was a prisoner, and he couldn't get the people in charge to listen to him. The centurion who was in charge of him was more inclined to listen to the helmsman and the owner of the ship. They said that the port they were in was not a good place to spend the winter, and they were sure that the weather would hold for them long enough to make it to a better port. There was a place further along the coast of Crete called Phoenix that would be much better. The majority on the ship agreed with them and Paul was overruled. They set sail again.

This aspect of Paul's situation is something that we can all relate to. You have been in situations where you felt in your spirit that God was telling you not to move in a certain direction, but because others were in charge, you had to go along. You felt a check in your spirit, but you were ignored. Paul's experience demonstrates that it is not a hopeless situation. You might just need to go on a fast.

Contrary to Paul's advice, they set out again. They had a gentle wind for a time and they thought that they were going to be fine. But it wasn't long before a strong wind started blowing that turned into a major storm. It got so strong that they couldn't sail into the wind anymore and had to turn downwind and let the storm carry them along.

Day after day, the ship struggled in the heavy storm. They threw much of the cargo overboard to make the ship lighter. They did everything that they knew to save the ship from being destroyed. They ran ropes underneath the hull to strengthen it against the pounding of the waves. They put out a sea anchor, a device that created a drag in the water so that they wouldn't move as fast with the wind. After many days, the crew and most of the passengers were ready to quit: "When neither sun nor stars appeared for many days and the storm continued raging, we finally gave up all hope of being saved" (Acts 27:20 NIV).

While all of this was going on, they were fasting. They had eaten nothing for many days at that point, which is, by definition, fasting. For Paul, it was a time of fasting and prayer. Even though he had felt in his spirit that they would lose their lives if they sailed, he still sought God's will and he was still praying for God to intervene. "After the men had gone a long time without food, Paul stood up before them and said: 'Men, you should have taken my advice not to sail from Crete; then you would have spared yourselves this damage and loss'" (Acts 27:21 NIV).

As with the other fasts and prayer that we have examined, this again opened the door to the supernatural and an angel showed up. It resulted in deliverance from the circumstances.

> "But now I urge you to keep up your courage, because not one of you will be lost; only the ship will be destroyed. Last night an angel of the God whose I am and whom I serve stood beside me and said, 'Do not be afraid, Paul. You must stand trial before Caesar; and God has graciously given you the lives of all who sail with you'" (Acts 27:22-24 NIV).

By that time, they had been on a fourteen-day fast. They found the wind driving them directly into the island of Malta. It was night, but they realized that they were nearing shore and they dropped anchors to keep from running aground. All they could do was hang on right there until morning. They were afraid that in the dark, they would run into rocks on the shore and completely destroy the ship.

By that time, everyone was willing to listen to Paul. Even though he was a prisoner, he virtually took charge. At one point, the sailors decided to abandon the ship and the passengers. They started to lower a lifeboat, claiming that they were going to take another anchor out away from the boat. Paul told the Roman centurion that if they were allowed to go, the rest of the passengers on the ship would die. This time the centurion acted on what Paul said.

Then Paul encouraged everyone to eat something so that they would have strength for the next morning:

> "And as day was about to dawn. Paul implored them all to take food, saying. Today is the fourteenth day you have waited and continued without food, and eaten nothing. Therefore I urge you to take nourishment, for this is for your survival, since not a hair will fall from the head of any of you. And when he had said these things, he took bread and gave thanks to God in the presence of them all; and when he had broken it he began to eat. Then they were all encouraged, and also took food themselves" (Acts 27:33-36).

When daylight came, they were able to get everyone onto the shore before the ship broke up. Just as the angel had said, the ship and cargo were lost, but all of the crew and passengers were spared. Altogether, there were 276 people on the ship whose lives were saved.

Fasting with prayer got rid of all doubt and unbelief. Notice that with three of the fasts we have studied so far—Daniel, Cornelius and Paul—the supernatural showed up. With the doubt and unbelief cleansed from them and their faith pure, the supernatural came on their behalf. When you have pure faith and you are in agreement with the supernatural, miraculous things happen. Nothing is impossible when you are in that place.

At times, we all miss God. We get a check in our spirit and we go ahead anyway, or we do something we shouldn't do. Sometimes, as with Paul, it is not our decision to make and we have no choice but to go in the direction that we think is wrong. It is good to know that with our faith purified through fasting with prayer, the impossible can still be accomplished.

When Tom and I first moved to Arizona, we were looking for a house. We were basically young country people moving to the big city and we had much to learn. We became associated with a realtor who saw how naive we were and he took full advantage of us. We found a house that he convinced us was ideal. At the time, we felt a check in our spirits, but everything in the natural looked fine, so we went with what the realtor said.

Needless to say, we ended up in a mess. We had been tricked into signing a deal that was not at all what we had been led to believe, and there was no way out of it. It wasn't long before we lost all hope in that situation. We knew that we had missed God, that we blew it. Now we had to face the consequences and we didn't exactly have strong faith that it would turn out okay.

In the midst of such discouragement, the natural tendency is to feel that we deserve to get beat up. It is our fault. But God can deliver, even in that type of situation. That was basically the situation Paul was in. It was hopeless. They all knew that Paul had told them they would die if they didn't listen to him. Now it looked as though his words were accurate. They had missed God and now they had to suffer the consequences. That is the time to go on a fast.

That is what Tom and I did. Rather than give in to the discouragement, we chose to fast and pray. We couldn't seem to sell the house. We couldn't find a way out of the situation. We knew we were not in the will of God. So we fasted and prayed and, as our faith became pure, God miraculously delivered us from that situation and blessed us.

When we repent and come before God, He is ready to rescue us, no matter what the situation is. It is not a matter of changing God. The fasting changes us. It changes our direction. It brings us into agreement with God and it brings us into the supernatural.

Fasting brings supernatural deliverance even when we are going in the wrong direction. It can get us back into the perfect will of God.

Summary

1. Paul was a prisoner being escorted from Israel to Rome by ship. He felt strongly that they should not sail, but he was overruled by others.
2. He could not control the situation. Because of the decisions of others, he was subjected to great danger.
3. Fasting and prayer brought the intervention of the supernatural on Paul's behalf. An angel came and spoke to him.

4. Paul's prayer and fasting affected others. It saved the lives of everyone on the ship.

5. The intervention of the supernatural that resulted from prayer and fasting elevated Paul from the status of a prisoner to a place of leadership. Everyone started looking to him for direction. The doubt and unbelief of the entire ship, both crew and passengers, were cleansed away.

6. Fasting and prayer brings deliverance and changes our direction.

Application

1. If you feel that you are in a situation that you have no control over, write it down in your journal. Surrender the situation to God and expect Him to bring deliverance. Receive your deliverance now.

2. Continue your daily Confessions. Add the following:

God causes all things work together for my good. (Romans 8:28)

I am able to minister to others, bless others, and do the work of the Lord. (Acts 13:2, Matthew 6:17-18)

I am victorious over sin.

I am receiving direction and protection.

8

Overcoming Rejection

If anyone ever had a reason to give up, it was David. At a very early age, his own family made him feel rejected. The prophet Samuel sent notice to David's father, Jesse, that he was coming to the house to anoint one of his sons as the king of Israel. Samuel had been the most prominent leader in Israel for many years. Having him come to your house was like getting a call from the president of the United States to tell you that he is dropping by to make one of your sons the next president. Naturally, Jesse wanted everything to be just right. Except he did not invite David to be there. He got all of his other children ready, but David was left out in the field, watching the sheep.

We don't know exactly what it was that Jesse had against his youngest son, but David's brothers felt the same thing. On one occasion, for example, three of David's brothers were with the army as they faced the Philistines. Jesse sent David to the front lines to see how his brothers were doing. While there, David expressed his opinion about the Philistine, Goliath, wondering why no one challenged him. David's brother turned on him. "Now Eliab his oldest brother heard when he spoke to the men; and Eliab's anger was aroused against David, and he said. 'Why did you come down here? And with whom have you left those few sheep in the wilderness? I know your pride and the insolence of your heart for you have come down to see the battle'" (1 Samuel 17:28).

That was typical of the attitude of David's brothers. It's not hard to guess at how David must have felt as a child, knowing that he was despised by his family.

But in spite of that, even though he was left out when Samuel came to visit, it was David whom Samuel wanted to see. It was David who was anointed to be the king. God accepted David. He saw David as valuable, even though David's own father did not.

From that time, David went on to serve King Saul as a young man. He became a part of Saul's inner circle, ministering to him by playing the harp when Saul was disturbed by a tormenting spirit. He developed a very close relationship with Saul. Saul became a father figure to him. After he killed Goliath, Saul made David his armor bearer and gave him his own daughter as a wife. David's leadership abilities were recognized and rewarded. David must have felt that he finally was in a place where his value was really appreciated.

But then something happened in Saul and all of a sudden, he became jealous of David's success and his popularity. Instead of valuing David, he tried to kill him—several times. David was forced into the whole cycle of rejection again, the same feeling of worthlessness. In fact, it was even worse this time, since David now had to flee for his life into the wilderness. It was no longer just his family, now the entire nation had turned against David.

This illustrates a problem that many of us have faced. Your parents are the spiritual covering over you. What they declare over you during your childhood stays with you for your entire life—whether good or bad—unless you do something to change it. If they rejected you or spoke worthlessness over you, then you will struggle with that as long as you live, unless you do something about it. David recognized how important this was in his own life, so he took steps to get rid of the rejection.

The real turning point came at the end of Saul's life. Saul was killed in battle along with his sons. Suddenly, all of Israel was threatened by the Philistines. It was a nation without leadership and under siege. Israel was in great peril.

There were some valiant men who rose to the occasion. They looked for Saul's body and buried it, but rather than panic or just give up, they chose to do something that would purify their faith so that the supernatural would come to their aid. God would move on behalf of the nation.

"Now when the inhabitants of Jabesh Gilead heard what the Philistines had done to Saul, all the valiant men arose and traveled all night, and took the body of Saul and the bodies of his sons from the wall of Beth Shan; and they came to Jabesh and burned them there. Then they took their bones and buried them under the tamarisk tree at Jabesh, and fasted seven days" (1 Samuel 31:11-13).

They fasted and prayed. But they were not the only ones. At the time, David was living in Philistine lands. He first heard about Saul's death from a man who had been there to see it. It was a critical moment for David. He had been anointed to be king, and it looked like this would be the perfect opportunity to step into that role. But there was still the rejection of a lifetime to overcome. We see that David did not rejoice in Saul's death. Rather, he went into mourning-and he fasted.

"Therefore David took hold of his own clothes and tore them, and so did all the men who were with him. And they mourned and wept and fasted until evening for Saul and for Jonathan his son, for the people of the LORD and for the house of Israel, because they had fallen by the sword" (2 Samuel 1:11-12).

By fasting, David got rid of any doubt and unbelief that would have interfered with stepping into his destiny. He could have sent a message to all of the tribes and told them, "I was anointed to be king and now I'm going to take the throne." The problem was that there were many who would have opposed him if he had done it that way. Instead, he waited on God so that he would have mustard seed faith, and he would act in wisdom instead of pride or revenge. All of the activity of the enemy throughout his life, the curse that his father had put on him, was broken.

David needed that faith to sustain him. There was a long civil war after that before everyone accepted David as the king. But not only did David become stronger each day, the Philistines were never able to take advantage of the discord in Israel. God's hand not only brought David's destiny to pass, but He protected the nation as well. David was prepared to be the leader of the nation because he put the welfare of all the tribes ahead of his own glory. He fasted and prayed for the nation. God honored him and brought him to the throne.

If you have experienced things in your life that seem to be holding you back, curses or worthlessness that your parents might have spoken over you, it may be that you need to fast in order to break free. If you know the destiny that God has called you to, but you just can't seem to get there, then you need to do what David did. Fasting brings you into the supernatural and eliminates that which stands in the way of your destiny.

When Tom and I entered the ministry, we began to realize how many things in our past were obstacles to our future. We had struggles with things that in the natural, we didn't seem to have any real control over. For example, divorce ran in both of our families. We could trace it back for many generations. That spirit had attached itself to us, and we were destined to be divorced. Through fasting and prayer, however, we not only identified that generational curse, but the supernatural came into our lives and broke it.

There were times early in our marriage when we struggled with money. We overcame the mentality of poverty by filling ourselves with the Word of God and then fasting and praying every time we experienced a crisis.

In fact, every struggle we have faced in our marriage and in our ministry has been overcome through prayer and fasting. We search the Scriptures and get the promises of God. We confess the Word and fill ourselves with it. But then we fast and pray so that our faith, our ability to believe what the Word of God says, is purified. With pure faith, the supernatural destroys every obstacle and then we can begin walking in the blessings of God.

Fasting with prayer breaks generational curses over your life and puts you in the position of an overcomer, victorious and blessed.

Summary

1. David had to overcome great rejection in his life:
   - from his family
   - from Saul
   - from the entire nation under Saul.
2. David knew he was anointed to be king, and he knew he had to overcome rejection. When he heard of Saul's death, he prepared for the next phase of his life by fasting.
3. Fasting and prayer eliminated all doubt that David might have experienced because of a lifetime of

rejection. He eliminated anything that would hinder the fulfillment of his destiny.

- He overcame rejection.
- He overcame his enemies.

Application

1. In your journal, list every part of your life that has caused you to feel rejected or has made you feel that you are a failure. Turn those areas over to God and allow Him to bring healing to those areas of your life. It may be that you are living under a generational curse. If so, commit that to the Lord as an area that you expect your fast to break.

2. Continue your daily Confessions.

9

Under Our Feet

*W*e can see how important fasting is by the fact that Jesus fasted. At the very beginning of His ministry, He went on a forty-day fast, before He did anything else. He certainly had pure faith already. He was completely without sin and had the most pure faith of anyone in history. Yet even Jesus found benefit from fasting. That should tell us that it is good for us to fast as well.

When we look at the reason for Jesus' fast, we see another benefit that we can have. Jesus fasted to put the enemy under His feet. Jesus was one hundred percent God, but He was also one hundred percent man—a perfect man. There was no sin in His life. He was pure, but to make sure that the appetites of His body did not run His life, Jesus fasted. Understand that the appetites are not evil. They are healthy appetites that we need for life, but they are not to control us. Jesus kept them in submission.

Jesus had just been baptized in the Jordan River. It was the beginning of His public ministry. He was on the verge of fulfilling His destiny, His calling. The first thing He did was to get away by Himself to fast and pray for forty days. That time prepared Him for the next part of His life.

At the end of forty days, Jesus was hungry. The enemy came to try to crush Him before He even got started. Satan's first attack tried to take advantage of Jesus' hunger: "Now when the tempter came to Him, he said, 'If You are the Son of God, command that these stones become bread'" (Matthew 4:3).

Jesus answered according the Word of God, not His appetites. "But He answered and said, 'It is written, "Man shall not live by bread alone, but by every word that proceeds from the mouth of God"'" (Matthew 4:4).

Jesus said, "No," to the physical body, the appetites of the body. He said, "I have control over food. Food will not have power over Me."

For many, that motive alone would be reason enough to fast. If you can't say, "No," to a piece of pie or cake or to soft drinks, then you need to break the power that food has over your life. You should have power over food. It should not have power over you. Jesus made sure that He was in charge, not His appetite. Fasting put Him in that position.

Next, the devil took Jesus up to the pinnacle of the Temple and told Him to throw Himself down. "Then the devil took Him up into the holy city, set Him on the pinnacle of the temple, and said to Him, 'If You are the Son of God, throw Yourself down.

For it is written: "He shall give His angels charge over you," and, "In their hands they shall bear you up, Lest you dash your foot against a stone"'" (Matthew 4:5-6).

Again, Jesus responded with the Word. "Jesus said to him, 'It is written again. "You shall not tempt the LORD your God"'" (Matthew 4:7).

The devil couldn't get Jesus to respond to physical appetites, so he tried to destroy Jesus by getting Him to do something foolish. He wanted Jesus to throw Himself down as though He was committing suicide. He quoted Scripture to Jesus to try to justify the act, but there was absolutely no reason for Jesus to do it. It would have been a foolish act.

Foolish actions can cost you your life. I spoke with someone recently who had burns all over his face and hands. The man's wife explained how it happened. His father was a pilot. He constantly said to him, "Pilots who take risks die young. So don't ever take a risk when you fly a plane."

One night, however, as he and his father flew into a small town airport, the runway lights didn't come on. They had plenty of fuel and they could have turned around and found another airport where they could have landed safely, but they had been flying all day and they were tired. The man's father was now seventy years old and he felt that he was just too tired to turn around. He just wanted to land the plane. In that moment, he made a foolish decision. He decided to land without lights.

The plane crashed. The father died and the son ended up with severe burns. A foolish action brought fatal consequences.

Jesus took the territory for us. We can look at His fast and the victory over the enemy that He gained, and we can believe that we will come under the anointing and believe that we are not going to do something foolish. Jesus broke the power of doing anything that would tempt God.

Jesus also gained victory over another area in His encounter with the devil. Satan, having failed twice already, tried one more time. He took Jesus up to the top of a very high mountain. "Again, the devil took Him up on an exceedingly high mountain, and showed Him all the kingdoms of the world and their glory. And he said to Him, 'All these things I will give You if You will fall down and worship me'" (Matthew 4:8-9).

As with the first two temptations, Jesus responded with the Word. "Then Jesus said to him, 'Away with you, Satan! For it is written, "You shall worship the Lord your God, and Him only you shall serve"'" (Matthew 4:10).

Sometimes we just want to worship ourselves. We want to serve "Me." It happens when we know that we should be doing something that God wants us to do, but we feel tired, so we don't want to do it. We feel the need to take time for ourselves.

Jesus overcame all of that. He declared that He would only serve God. He would only worship God. He would only speak the words that God told Him to speak.

There are times that the flesh becomes our greatest obstacle to fulfilling our destinies. When we first started the church, we went day and night, praying and fasting. We fasted with prayer every week. There was always something coming up and Tom would say, "We have to fast. Call the elders and the pastors."

There was a tremendous amount of work to do and after a while, I got to the point that I didn't want to see anyone. We would get home and I was done. I didn't want to be bothered by anyone or anything else. I would look at Tom and say, "I'm so depressed right now."

Of course, I wanted to hear, "You're in burnout. You need to take a break. Just rest a little, you poor thing." I wanted sympathy.

But Tom didn't say that. He just looked at me and said, "You just ran smack into self, didn't you?"

I'd be a little upset for a day or so, and then I would say, "Okay, God, I ran smack into self. I repent. This is sin. I need to go to the next level."

All of the depression and oppression would lift right off of me, and I was again ready to run the race. I didn't surrender to the word "burnout." Tom wouldn't let me. I was able to die to self and go on to what God wanted in my life.

Jesus, by refusing to worship anything but God, by not giving in to self and hunger or tiredness, overcame burnout.

Jesus took all of these territories and put the enemy under His feet. He overcame the power of food and the desires of the flesh. He overcame doing foolish things and He overcame the worship of self.

Fasting was a part of His victory over Satan. At the end of the forty days, Satan was under Jesus' feet.

Summary

1. Even Jesus, who had the most pure faith of anyone in history, found benefit in fasting. After His baptism, before He started His public ministry, He went into the wilderness to fast for forty days.

2. Jesus fasted to put Satan under His feet. He dealt with every temptation that the devil could throw at Him:

   a. He said, "No," to the appetites of the body.

   b. He said, "No," to foolish acts.

   c. He overcame the worship of self.

3. Fasting will overcome the same things in our lives. It will break any habit that we have struggled with. It will bring us wisdom so that we don't do foolish things. It will overcome the worship of ourselves.

Application

1. In your journal, list the areas that have always been problems to you. Ask yourself these questions:

   a. Is there some habit that you have not been able to overcome?

   b. Have you made foolish decisions in the past that got you into trouble?

   c. Do you have great pride in your own abilities or accomplishments?

2. Now that you can recognize those areas as problems that are keeping you from experiencing the blessings of God, ask forgiveness for each of them. Receive forgiveness and commit yourself to allowing God to change you so that you will be completely free. Allow the fast to cleanse doubt and unbelief from you and to break the hold that those things had on you.

3. Continue your daily Confessions.

10

Facing the Bully

om and I have fasted often in our Christian lives. Every time that we felt stuck and we couldn't seem to get to the next level that God had for us, even though we quoted the Word and meditated on it, we went on a fast. As our faith was purified, we overcame every kind of obstacle, and we have seen the will of God fulfilled in our lives.

One significant thing that fasting with prayer helps us gain victory over is fear. We have all faced situations or people who have set themselves against us that have caused great fear to rise up in us. God does not intend for you to be defeated by anything. You have not been given a spirit of fear, but of power, love and a sound mind. You need to eliminate fear from your life. Fasting with prayer can cleanse fear out of your faith.

Near the end of the book of Judges, there is a story that is as bizarre as it is disturbing. It describes an incident that led to a civil war in Israel between the tribe of Benjamin and the other eleven tribes. Before it was finished, fasting with prayer played a significant role in overcoming fear. The story is described in Judges 19 and 20.

There was a Levite from the mountains of Ephraim who traveled to Bethlehem, in the southern part of Israel. On the return trip, accompanied by his concubine and a servant, he found himself in the vicinity of Jerusalem as it was approaching nightfall. This was before the time when David made Jerusalem the capital of Israel. It was still a Gentile city and the Levite decided to travel on to Gibeah a few miles away, a city inhabited by people from the tribe of Benjamin.

The Levite found no place there to stay, so he and his two companions went into the open square in the middle of the city and tried to make themselves as comfortable as possible. As they were settling in, an old man saw them and invited them to spend the night at his house. They accepted and the old man entertained them that night. Everyone was having a pleasant evening.

The Benjamites were known for being fierce and aggressive. When Jacob prayed over his sons before his death, he prophesied that Benjamin would be "a ravenous wolf," who would "devour the prey" in the morning, "and at night he shall divide the spoil" (Genesis 49:27). Benjamin's descendants were known by that reputation. They were bullies. The other tribes were afraid of them.

In the story of the Levite and his concubine, the Benjamites certainly lived up to their reputation. A gang of perverted men of the city came to the house and demanded that the Levite be sent out to them so they could have sex with him.

The owner of the house pleaded with them not to abuse his guest. He offered to send out his daughter and the Levite's concubine instead, but they persisted in their demand. Finally the concubine was sent out to them and the men of the town abused her violently all night. When morning came, they left her alone. She crawled up to the door of the house and died.

When the Levite went outside, he found his concubine dead on the doorstep. He placed the concubine's body on his donkey and returned to his home in Ephraim. Then he decided to make this crime known to all of Israel by doing something unorthodox.

"When he entered his house he took a knife, laid hold of his concubine, and divided her into twelve pieces, limb by limb, and sent her throughout all the territory of Israel. And so it was that all who saw it said, 'No such deed has been done or seen from the day that the children of Israel came up from the land of Egypt until this day. Consider it, confer, and speak up!'" (Judges 19:29-30).

Everyone was horrified. No atrocity like that had ever been committed before. It wasn't just the terrible nature of the crime, however, that caused alarm.

There was a curse that came with the shedding of innocent blood. The land was not to be defiled in the way that the Gentiles had done before Israel lived there. The result of defiling the land was to be kicked out of the land. "...lest the land vomit you out also when you defile it, as it vomited out the nations that were before you" (Leviticus 18:28).

Defilement of the land came from sin. One of the most serious of those sins was the shedding of innocent blood. No mercy was to be shown to the one who committed the crime of murder of an innocent person.

> "..lest innocent blood be shed in the midst of your land which the LORD your God is giving you as an inheritance, and thus the guilt of bloodshed be upon you. But if anyone hates his neighbor, lies in wait for him, rises against him and strikes him mortally, so that he dies, and he flees to one of these cities, then the elders of his city shall send and bring him from there, and deliver him over to the hand of the avenger of blood, that he may die. Your eye shall not pity him, but you shall put away the guilt of innocent blood from Israel, that it may go well with you" (Deuteronomy 19:10-13).

Innocent blood had been shed by Benjamin, and it needed to be dealt with or the land would be cursed. The news spread through the eleven tribes, and they gathered together to discuss the problem. It was decided unanimously that they needed to take action. They formed an army and prepared to attack the city of Gibeah. They sent a message, demanding that the men be surrendered who had committed the crime.

The problem was that the Benjamites were a fierce and savage people who had no intention of submitting to the demands of anyone. Instead of surrendering the criminals, they formed an army to defend themselves.

It should have been a lopsided battle. Benjamin only had a little over 26,000 men to face 400,000 from the rest of Israel. However, fear played a big part in the outcome, a fear that came from doubt and unbelief. Israel didn't really believe that Benjamin could be defeated. They went before God and didn't even ask if they were going to win or how they should win. They just asked who should go first into battle. God told them to send Judah.

The battle was a disaster. Israel lost 22,000 men that day as they were severely defeated by a much smaller army. The savage, wolf-like ferocity of Benjamin won the day.

Israel wept before God that night. They lost sight of the original goal of ridding the land of the curse and were ready to give up. They asked God if they should even bother to attack again. They still outnumbered Benjamin by an overwhelming margin, but the fear was stronger than ever. God told them to try again. "Then the children of Israel went up and wept before the LORD until evening, and asked counsel of the LORD, saying, 'Shall I again draw near for battle against the children of my brother Benjamin?' And the LORD said, 'Go up against him'" (Judges 20:23).

The next day, Israel marched up just as they had the day before-and were soundly beaten, just as they had been the day before. Numbers were on their side. They were fighting for what was right. They had all the advantages, but they couldn't get the victory. At that point, they decided to do what they should have done from the beginning. They went on a fast with prayer. "Then all the children of Israel, that is, all the people, went up and came to the house of God and wept. They sat there before the LORD and fasted that day until evening; and they offered burnt offerings and peace offerings before the LORD" (Judges 20:26).

In a fast, God gives direction for what is needed to bring the victory. By fasting with prayer, Israel got rid of their doubt and unbelief and God gave them a plan.

The next day, they set an ambush. They attacked as before and retreated as before, but this time it was a ruse, not a defeat. The Benjamites chased them as before and left the city unprotected. Once the defenders were gone, the men in ambush attacked the city and Benjamin was defeated. The innocent blood was avenged and the curse on the land was lifted.

This story illustrates how fasting can be used to eliminate fear in your life. If you have an enemy who is a bully or if there is a situation in your life that causes fear, that fear will keep you from victory. Fasting will bring you into mustard-seed faith, free from doubt and unbelief, and drive out the fear. God is greater than any fear that you might have. Use fasting to cleanse fear out of your life and bring you to victory.

Summary

1. Fasting and prayer will help you gain victory over fear, cleansing it out of your life. The incident described in Judges 19 and 20 is an example of fasting to overcome fear.

2. A Levite stayed the night in the town of Gibeah, a town of the tribe of Benjamin. While there, his concubine was raped and killed. The other tribes gathered an army to attack Benjamin and demand that the perpetrators of the crime be dealt with so that the land would not be defiled by innocent blood. Benjamin refused and gathered its own army.
3. Benjamin was a tribe noted for its ferocity. Even though outnumbered, they still won two battles.
4. The other tribes fasted and prayed to cleanse fear from their army. Only when the doubt and unbelief were removed were they able to win the next battle.

Application

1. Do you experience fear in your life? It might be fear of failure, fear of not being accepted, or fear of rejection. There are many kinds of fear. If you experience fear, it will keep you from exercising your faith and entering into the blessings that God has for you. Write every fear that you struggle with in your journal. As you write them down, commit them to God and receive deliverance from them.
2. Continue your daily Confessions. Add the following:

I have not been given a spirit of fear, but of power and love and a sound mind. (2 Timothy 1:7)

11

The Proclaimed Fast

I have spent most of my life confessing the Word of God and living in God's promises. I have experienced miraculous healing several times. I have a very healthy diet and I take good care of myself.

In spite of all this, however, there came a point where my health just started failing. Every time I went to the doctor, I got another bad report. So I would confess the Word and prop myself back up and keep going. It eventually began to wear me down, however. I felt like I was losing the fight. I was nearly ready to surrender and just give up.

I began to confess healing Scripture even more. I knew I couldn't just quit, even though I wanted to, because my body is the temple of the Holy Spirit. It is not my own. I knew that I had been bought by the blood of Jesus and that by His stripes, I was healed.

As I was going through this time of struggle, the Holy Spirit began to show me some things about my family. I realized that on my father's side, my ancestors didn't live beyond their sixties. And I was getting close to sixty. I was under a generational curse. There was something there that needed to be dealt with or I would die in my sixties, just like the rest of my family. I went on a long fast with prayer.

Things changed while I was on that fast. Ever since that time, I have felt better than I did in my twenties. I am more energetic than I've ever been. Every doctor's report that I get now says that I am very healthy. A year after that fast, I did a number of tests. I ran on a treadmill and the doctor commented that my heart was in great condition. He thought I would probably live for another hundred years. I agreed.

Then I had a bone density test. The last time I had that test, it showed that my bones were terrible. I was told that I had osteoporosis, which is a crippling, incurable disease that causes bones to deteriorate. This time, however, the nurse told me that I had excellent bones. There was no bone loss at all. Bones don't fix themselves. Only God can do that, and according to Isaiah 58:11, He does. It was a miracle.

While I was fasting, the seventy-five percent of my energy that was normally used for digesting food was redirected to repairing everything that was wrong in my body. The miraculous came into my life and eliminated the curse. I will now outlive my ancestors. I will live well past my sixties. I feel better now than I did in my twenties. Fasting with prayer brought deliverance from that generational curse and restored my health.

There are different types of fasts. What I just described is called a proclaimed fast. By that, I mean a fast that you proclaim because you feel that you need it. It is not something that God tells you to do. You determine that you need it.

For years, I didn't fast because I was waiting for the Holy Spirit to tell me to fast. I didn't want to do anything out of God's will. There were times when He did tell me, but there were many other times when I didn't hear God speak. I felt like I needed to fast, but I was afraid of getting under the law, so I waited for the Holy Spirit to tell me to fast.

As I began to study the Word of God about fasting, however, I discovered the proclaimed fast. I realized that I didn't need to wait for a word from God. If I was in a crisis, and I needed to cleanse doubt and unbelief from my life, I could proclaim a fast and start to move into the miraculous. Now, if I receive bad news, I don't have to wait for a specific word from God. I can choose to fast. This is what happened with the people that we have studied so far. Daniel, for example, was in a time of crisis. Fasting was appropriate.

Anytime that you find yourself confronted with any kind of crisis, you need to have pure faith, and the best way to get that is to cleanse yourself of doubt and unbelief through a fast. In fact, fasting will often mean the difference between victory and defeat. The doctor tells you that you have a terminal disease; you need to fast. You find that you are going to lose your job; it is time to go on a fast. You have problems with your children; get into pure faith by fasting. Mustard-seed faith at the moment of the crisis is vital. It pleases God when you determine to sacrifice food in order to get into pure mustard-seed faith.

The proclaimed fast opens up the miraculous. It cleanses us from doubt and unbelief and it frees us to override the natural laws that are around us. On a proclaimed fast, we need to hear from God. We need God to do something. The fast with prayer gives us victory over sin in our lives. It frees us from generational curses. It gives direction and protection and overrules every attempt of the enemy to attack us.

Jehoshaphat Confronting His Fear

It was in response to an attack by a powerful enemy that King Jehoshaphat proclaimed a fast. This is a story that is familiar to most of us. However, when we have looked at this story, we have usually focused on the power of praise and worship. We love to skip over the first part of the story and talk about how singers went out before the army and God gave a great victory through worship. I want you to see, however, the part that a proclaimed fast played in Jehoshaphat's reaction to the crisis. I believe this story has been very misunderstood.

The crisis came when the people of Moab, Ammon and others marched to attack Jerusalem. Word came to Jehoshaphat that this multitude was already on its way. They were at En Gedi, within thirty miles of the city. There wasn't much time to get ready. Jehoshaphat reacted immediately after he heard the news. "And Jehoshaphat feared, and set himself to seek the LORD, and proclaimed a fast throughout all Judah" (2 Chronicles 20:3).

It is worth noting that the first reaction was fear. That is a common thing for all of us. When we are confronted with bad news, we feel fear. The question is, what will we do when we feel the fear? Will we let it control us, or will we react the way Jehoshaphat did?

Instead of becoming paralyzed by the fear, Jehoshaphat took action. He did the one thing that he knew would be effective. He proclaimed a fast. He didn't deny the fear. He just realized that he needed to get rid of it. He had to get out of the doubt and the unbelief and get into faith. He had to move into the place of mustard-seed faith, where nothing would be impossible. He set himself to seek the Lord and the way to do that was through a fast. He proclaimed a fast for all of Judah.

After the fast was proclaimed, the entire nation sought the Lord. "So Judah gathered together to ask help from the LORD; and from all the cities of Judah they came to seek the LORD" (2 Chronicles 20:4).

Don't Neglect Prayer

Judah asked God for help. They prayed. Fasting is actually nothing more than going without food. If you're not praying and seeking God while you are on the fast, then it is not a spiritual fast. It will still have health benefits, but you need to combine prayer with your fasting.

As they prayed, Jehoshaphat stood up and spoke to the people. Instead of speaking from the fear that he felt, he began to agree with God and declare what God had said. "O LORD

God of our fathers, are You not God in heaven, and do You not rule over all the kingdoms of the nations, and in Your hand is there not power and might, so that no one is able to withstand You?" (2 Chronicles 20:6).

Jehoshaphat proclaimed that God was more powerful than the army coming against them, that no enemy could stand against God. Jehoshaphat spoke a confession of faith. No matter what the circumstances looked like, he looked into the unseen and brought himself into alignment with the Word of God.

As you face a crisis in your life, it is important that you do not come into agreement with the fear that you feel. Don't come into agreement with the garbage that comes up. When you fast, in the natural realm, all those toxins go into your bloodstream and you feel terrible. The more toxins there are, the more miserable you will feel. You will want to crawl into bed and pull the covers over your head and not move until the fast is over.

The same thing happens in the spiritual. The toxins of doubt and unbelief start to come up. The things in your life that are keeping you from faith start to rise to the surface. The more doubt and unbelief you have, the more garbage that will come up. That is the stuff that you have to get rid of. Don't be surprised by what comes up in you while you are fasting. You need to get rid of it. Don't come into agreement with it. Agree with the Word of God instead. Step out of the doubt and unbelief. Renounce it. Curse it at the root. Ask God to take it out of you, to wash it away. Fasting is for cleansing those things from your life. Stay in agreement with God and let the fast do its cleansing work.

Jehoshaphat had a distinct purpose that he declared for the fast. He wanted to change the circumstances. He had to destroy the power of fear. The fast was to destroy the destruction that was coming. It was to defeat the discouragement. It was to put the enemy under his feet.

When you encounter a crisis, you cannot have fear in your life. You cannot allow dismay or discouragement. You have to be in agreement with the Holy Spirit and be full of boldness and courage. The fast will pull down all of those strongholds that oppose God's destiny in your life. Jehoshaphat felt fear, but he took steps to get rid of it. The people fasted and they sought the Lord.

Receive a Word from God

As Judah aligned themselves with the Word of God, they were able to move into faith. They got a word from God. A man named Jahaziel stood in the midst of the people and spoke. "And he said, 'Listen, all you of Judah and you inhabitants of Jerusalem, and you, King Jehoshaphat! Thus says the LORD to you: "Do not be afraid nor dismayed because of this great multitude, for the battle is not yours, but God's"'" (2 Chronicles 20:15)

They heard from God. They were now in faith and they could let go, trust God and He would protect and defend them. They had a living word from the Lord. God was their protector.

No matter what crisis we might face, when we move into faith, we find that God is ready to fight the battle for us. He always tells us not to identify with the fear. Every great man of

God in the Bible had to choose between fear and the Word of God. Every time they aligned themselves with the Word, God told them not to fear. He would be their protector.

Abram had to face fear. Great kings of the land captured Abram's nephew, Lot, and Abram had to rescue him. Afterwards, there was the fear of what those nations would do to retaliate. But God spoke to Abram, "After these things the word of the LORD came to Abram in a vision, saying, 'Do not be afraid, Abram. I am your shield, your exceedingly great reward'" (Genesis 15:1).

In the New Testament, we are told not to try and avenge ourselves. That is God's place. "Beloved, do not avenge yourselves, but rather give place to wrath; for it is written, 'Vengeance is Mine, I will repay,' says the Lord" (Romans 12:19).

We have to get to a place where we can trust God and let go of the situation. We have to trust Him to protect us. Psalm 37 tells us not to fret because of evildoers, not to get anxious or worry about how things will turn out.

> Trust in the LORD, and do good;
>
> Dwell in the land, and feed on His faithfulness.
>
> Delight yourself also in the LORD,
>
> And He shall give you the desires of your heart.
>
> (Psalm 37:3-4)

Follow Faith with Worship

Jehoshaphat and the people of Judah moved out of fear and into faith. They fasted until they were cleansed of their doubt and unbelief and God stepped in and rescued them. They entered into mustard-seed faith, proclaimed what God said, made a confession of faith and then received a word from God. They let that word get planted in their hearts, and then they began to praise God.

"And Jehoshaphat bowed his head with his face to the ground, and all Judah and the inhabitants of Jerusalem bowed before the LORD, worshiping the LORD. Then the Levites of the children of the Kohathites and of the children of the Korahites stood up to praise the LORD God of Israel with voices loud and high" (2 Chronicles 20:18-19).

That is how faith works. When you receive the word that God has for you, you have it. Worship is an important part of the process. Your subconscious can't tell whether something you are talking about has already happened or if it's in the future. When you start to praise God and call it done, your subconscious moves right into faith. It assumes that you must have it now and it comes into complete agreement. It doesn't know any different. That is where faith happens.

The circumstances hadn't changed at all, but Israel knew they had the victory. God had promised to be their protection and fight the battle for them, so they received that and began to worship Him. It was done. The battle was won.

They set out the next morning to face the enemy. They continued in the same place of faith by putting singers in front of the army to sing to the Lord and to "praise the beauty of holiness" (verse 21). While they worshiped, God fought the battle.

"Now when they began to sing and to praise, the LORD set ambushes against the people of Ammon, Moab, and Mount Seir, who had come against Judah; and they were defeated. For the people of Ammon and Moab stood up against the inhabitants of Mount Seir to utterly kill and destroy them. And when they had made an end of the inhabitants of Seir, they helped to destroy one another" (2 Chronicles 20:22-23).

The enemy killed each other. The battle was over before Jehoshaphat and his army arrived. Then came the reward. They found an abundance of spoils, so much that it took three days to haul it all away.

The connection of fasting with abundant wealth is not often considered, but it is important. We have seen people who just can't seem to get out of poverty. They hear the prosperity message and they begin tithing. They seem to do the right things, but for some reason, they can't seem to get ahead.

The problem isn't that God doesn't want them to be blessed. More often, there is something that is keeping the blessing from reaching them and staying. My husband, Tom, will tell you that he grew up with a poverty mentality. His father worked hard, but he always made just enough to get by. That mentality had to be overcome. It was a generational curse of poverty in his life.

Whatever it is that might keep you from abundance and great wealth, it will probably be difficult to overcome on your own. It will look like an invincible army of circumstances that are keeping you poor. Just like Jehoshaphat, you have to begin by realizing that you are intimidated by the opposition. Then you must move from fear to faith by filling yourself with the Word and then purifying your faith through prayer and fasting.

That is what Tom and I did. We learned the promises of the Word that related to our finances. We filled ourselves constantly with the Word, confessing it and meditating on it. Then, whenever we ran into financial difficulties, we learned to fast and pray so that our faith could connect to the Word. The result is that today we live in great abundance. Wealth and increase came as the result of victory over the curses in our lives.

It all begins with a fast. The first thing Jehoshaphat felt was fear, but he refused to identify with it. Instead, he proclaimed a fast and cleansed the doubt and unbelief out of Israel. The result was complete victory and a supernatural reward.

A proclaimed fast in your life will have the same kind of result. No matter what the doctor said, no matter what the circumstance you are faced with, by fasting, you eliminate doubt and unbelief and you come into mustard-seed faith. From faith, you move into the realm of the supernatural where there is supernatural increase and supernatural blessing.

Summary

1. You don't have to wait for God to tell you to go on a fast. You can proclaim a fast simply because you think you need it.

2. Jehoshaphat proclaimed a fast and the story of his experience tells us some of the elements that we can incorporate in our own lives to make fasting and prayer more effective.

   a. Jehoshaphat's first reaction to the crisis was fear. He didn't deny the fear, but he refused to identify with it. He took action to get rid of it. He proclaimed a fast.

   b. Don't be surprised by what comes up in you while you are fasting. It is the toxins of doubt and unbelief that need to be cleansed from you.

   c. Jehoshaphat didn't neglect prayer. He sought God while fasting. He reminded God of all His promises. Jehoshaphat spoke a confession of faith.

   d. Jehoshaphat received a word from God while fasting. As a fast cleanses doubt and unbelief out of you, you move from fear to faith.

   e. Jehoshaphat and the people began to worship. Your subconscious can't tell whether something you are talking about happened in the past or the future. When you praise God and call it done, your subconscious moves into faith.

f. The miraculous came and Israel was delivered from the crisis. All they had to do was go out and collect the spoils.

Application

1. Review everything that you have written in your journal that represents obstacles to your destiny. Now begin a new list of times when God has brought you deliverance, healing, etc. Remind yourself of the times when God's power worked in your life. As you look at the new list, thank God for each time that He has moved on your behalf and begin to worship Him for doing the same with the problems that you face now.

2. As you continue your daily Confessions, allow the Word to bring you from fear to faith and know that fasting will purify that faith.

12

Pride and Prejudice

*I*n this modern age when we are dealing worldwide with the threat of terrorism, people often feel helpless to do anything. It seems like such a massive threat to our way of life that we wonder what one person can do. For many, that means passively accepting fate and living in fear of the future.

There is something that you can do, however. You can go on a proclaimed fast with prayer for the nation, a sacrificial fast for others. In times of national crisis, it is especially important that people take the time to seek God's supernatural intervention. Throughout the history of the United States, America's leaders have called on people to fast and pray for the nation, much as we saw Jehoshaphat do for Israel. For many years, it was a standard and regular practice of our leaders. As a result, God's hand has been on America from the beginning. Though few

Americans realize it today, fasting and prayer were part of our heritage two hundred years before the American Revolution.

The story of Esther is another example of how one person fasting with prayer can affect the destiny of an entire nation. It also demonstrates how fasting with prayer can free us from fear—fear of being destroyed, fear of failure and fear of prejudice.

Esther was a queen. She was a Jewish girl who, by the favor of God, had been brought to the attention of the ruler of the great Media-Persian Empire, King Ahasuerus. She was an orphan who had been raised by her uncle Mordecai. The king didn't know she was one of the Jewish exiles living in Persia. She had been among many young virgins from which he chose a wife to be his queen. Mordecai had advised Esther not to tell anyone of her background, so she had kept it a secret.

Mordecai frequently sat in the vicinity of the king's gate so that he could stay in touch with Esther. It was there that he became involved in an incident that God would later use for the benefit of the nation. Two of the king's eunuchs, Bigthan and Teresh, became angry with the king and plotted to assassinate him. Mordecai became aware of the plot and passed the information on to Esther, who told the king, and the two men were hung. As a result, Mordecai's name was written into the book of chronicles that recorded the history of the king's reign.

One of the prominent leaders of Persia was a man named Haman. The king liked him enough that he promoted him to the highest position in the land, second only to the king, and gave orders that everyone should bow to him and pay him homage.

The one person who refused to bow to Haman was Mordecai. When Haman passed through the gate, everyone bowed down except Mordecai. The officials at the gate asked him every day why he refused to give the same respect to Haman as everyone else. He told them that he would not bow because he was a Jew. That meant that, out of conscience, he could not give the kind of homage Haman wanted to anyone but God. The respect that Haman demanded of those around him went beyond the normal respect given to a ruler. He wanted worship. And Mordecai refused to do it.

When word got to Haman that Mordecai would not bow to him, he developed a hatred, not just for Mordecai, but for all Jews. He determined that he would get rid of the entire race. He began to plot a way to do it.

By casting lots, Haman determined the day that the Jews were to be destroyed. It was a date a few weeks away. Then he went before the king and, appealing to the king's pride through flattery, he manipulated him into agreeing to a law against the Jews.

"Then Haman said to King Ahasuerus, 'There is a certain people scattered and dispersed among the people in all the provinces of your kingdom; their laws are different from all other people's, and they do not keep the king's laws. Therefore it is not fitting for the king to let them remain. If it pleases the king, let a decree be written that they be destroyed, and I will pay ten thousand talents of silver into the hands of those who do the work, to bring it into the king's treasuries'" (Esther 3:8-9).

Haman convinced the king that the Jews were a serious threat to him, and the king agreed to let him get rid of them. He gave Haman his signet ring, symbol of the king's authority, and told him to do what seemed good to him. Haman sat down with the scribes and drafted a law that was sent out to all the provinces of Persia. "And the letters were sent by couriers into all the king's provinces, to destroy, to kill, and to annihilate all the Jews, both young and old, little children and women, in one day, on the thirteenth day of the twelfth month, which is the month of Adar, and to plunder their possessions" (Esther 3:13).

That settled it. In Persia, once the law went out, it could not be changed. It could not be revoked, even by the king. Haman would have his revenge.

When Mordecai heard what had happened, he put on sackcloth and ashes and cried out loudly in the midst of the city. In fact, Esther 4:3 says that everywhere the decree was read, the Jews began fasting and weeping.

Esther heard what Mordecai was doing and sent a servant to find out what the problem was. Mordecai arranged for her to see a copy of Haman's decree and told her about the money that Haman was willing to pay into the king's treasury to destroy the Jews. He sent word to Esther that she had to go into the king and plead for him to spare her people.

Esther immediately pointed out a problem with that plan. According to Persian law, no one could come before the king unless summoned, not even the queen. If she went into his presence unannounced, it could mean the death penalty for her. Only if the king held out his golden scepter to her, would her life be spared. She had not seen the king for thirty days and she could not just walk in without him calling for her. Mordecai was asking her to take a very great risk.

In response, Mordecai sent Esther a kind of ultimatum.

"And Mordecai told them to answer Esther: 'Do not think in your heart that you will escape in the king's palace any more than all the other Jews. For if you remain completely silent at this time, relief and deliverance will arise from the Jews from another place, but you and your father's house will perish. Yet who knows whether you have come to the kingdom for such a time as this?'" (Esther 4: 13-14).

This question is something that we all need to ask ourselves when we see evil in the land. Are we ready to do something about it? Are we willing to take the time to fast and pray for God to intervene? Maybe this is the destiny that God is calling you to. Perhaps you were born for "such a time as this." We are usually too willing to pass the buck and wait for someone else to do it.

That is the message that Mordecai sent to Esther. It may be that God put her in the position of queen just so she could take action at this moment.

Esther decided that Mordecai was right and that she needed to do something. Rather than just rush into the king's presence, however, she proclaimed a fast with prayer.

"Then Esther told them to reply to Mordecai: 'Go, gather all the Jews who are present in Shushan, and fast for me; neither eat nor drink for three days, night or day. My maids and I will fast likewise. And so I will go to the king, which is against the law; and if I perish, I perish!'" (Esther 4:15-16).

Esther made a commitment to her destiny. She decided to do something that could cost her life. If she didn't do it, it could cost the lives of all of her people in the kingdom. But she didn't just go do it. She prepared. She didn't just spend one night in prayer. She decided on a three-day fast to get rid of any doubt and unbelief. She wanted to move into mustard-seed faith in order to see God move in a miraculous way on her behalf.

After three days, Esther dressed herself in her royal robes, and made herself look as beautiful as she could. Then she went to the king's inner court. That was the moment that was critical. If the king was in a bad mood that day, he could easily have her executed. That was what the law said. He hadn't seen her for thirty days and he hadn't called for her to come on that day. She walked in, risking her life.

"So it was, when the king saw Queen Esther standing in the court, that she found favor in his sight, and the king held out to Esther the golden scepter that was in his hand. Then Esther went near and touched the top of the scepter" (Esther 5:2). God gave her favor. The king asked her what request she had from him. He was ready to grant her whatever she wanted at that moment, up to half the kingdom. She could ask for anything.

Esther had much wisdom in that situation. The fasting and prayer had given her great favor. Now she wanted to take full advantage of it. Instead of just blurting out what she wanted, she decided to pique the king's interest. She invited him to a banquet the next day, where she would make her request known. The king was completely hooked. The way that Esther put off telling him what she wanted made him all the more curious. Now he would hang on every word that she said. She gave him an entire day to think about it and wonder. By the time she presented her request, he would be completely ready to grant it.

Esther then showed what courage she had. She also invited Haman. Esther, who three days before had been hesitant to even go before the king, now was bold and assertive. She was ready to confront her enemy face to face. Fasting will make you courageous. It gets you out of the realm of fear. It eliminates discouragement and makes you bold.

Haman was excited to be invited to the queen's house for dinner. He considered it a great honor. His vanity made him believe that Esther wanted to pay him some special tribute. In his pride, he imagined all sorts of things.

Later that day, Haman saw Mordecai again, and still, Mordecai would not bow down to him. Haman was more indignant than ever, but he knew the day was coming when he could destroy Mordecai, so he didn't say anything. As he later met with his wife and some friends, however, he began complaining about how much he hated Mordecai. He bragged about the great riches and honor that the king had given him.

He had been promoted to a place of greater power than anyone else in the kingdom except the king. He had many children and great wealth. He had been invited to a dinner with just the king and queen. Yet, in spite of all this, he could not enjoy it. "Yet all this avails me nothing, so long as I see Mordecai the Jew sitting at the king's gate" (Esther 5:13).

Haman's friends suggested that he should build a gallows that night and, in the morning, suggest to the king that Mordecai should be hung on it that day, rather than waiting for the day when all the Jews were to be destroyed. While he had such favor with the king, his wish would surely be granted.

Haman loved the idea. He dispatched servants to begin the work and by the next morning, there was a gallows standing in front of Haman's house, fifty cubits high.

God was not finished, however. Esther and Mordecai had been fasting and the miraculous continued to happen. The king couldn't sleep that night. He couldn't stop wondering what Esther wanted. His curiosity kept him awake late.

To pass the time, he called for the book of the chronicles of his reign to be brought in and read to him. He loved to hear about what he had done.

His servants read to him through the night and into the morning. They came to the account of how Mordecai had saved the king's life. The king stopped them at that point and asked if anything had ever been done to honor Mordecai and thank him for his act of loyalty. They said that nothing had been done. The king decided that he needed to somehow thank Mordecai.

He asked who was in the court that he could discuss the matter with.

God's timing was perfect, as always. The only one in the court that morning was Haman. He had just come in with the intention of asking the king to hang Mordecai. Before he could present his request, however, the king asked him a question.

"So Haman came in, and the king asked him, 'What shall be done for the man whom the king delights to honor?'" (Esther 6:6). In his pride, Haman assumed that the king must be talking about him. Who else would the king want to honor so much? So he suggested an honor that he would enjoy.

"And Haman answered the king, 'For the man whom the king delights to honor, let a royal robe be brought which the king has worn, and a horse on which the king has ridden, which has a royal crest placed on its head. Then let this robe and horse be delivered to the hand of one of the king's most noble princes, that he may array the man whom the king delights to honor. Then parade him on horseback through the city square, and proclaim before him: "Thus shall it be done to the man whom the king delights to honor!"'" (Esther 6:7-9).

Haman fully expected the king to smile and say, "As you have spoken, it will be done for you." But instead, the king told him that he would be the noble prince who would take the honor to the man named Mordecai.

The king had no idea that Haman hated Mordecai and was about to ask permission to execute him. He had no idea that Mordecai was related to Esther. Haman had no idea when he walked into the king's court that he would have to go and honor Mordecai rather than kill him. He had to find Mordecai, give him the king's robe, put him on the king's horse and lead him through the city square, proclaiming, "Thus shall it be done to the man whom the king delights to honor!"

Haman felt utterly humiliated. After it was over, he went back to his house with his head covered in mourning. His wife and friends did little to console him. They told him that if Mordecai was prevailing over him, he was doomed to failure. In the midst of his despair, the king's servants arrived to escort him to Esther's banquet.

God knew the beginning from the end. He took what was a certain disaster for Mordecai and turned it into advancement and honor. But there was still the matter of Esther's request. Haman didn't know that Mordecai was related to Esther, either, and he had no idea what was coming.

They all arrived at the banquet. By this time, the king was all ears. He has been thinking about Esther's request all night and all day. He could hardly wait. At last the moment arrived, and Esther agreed to tell him what she wanted. At that point, with Haman listening, she asked the king for her life.

"Then Queen Esther answered and said, 'If I have found favor in your sight, O king, and if it pleases the king, let my life be given me at my petition, and my people at my request. For we have been sold, my people and I, to be destroyed, to be killed, and to be annihilated. Had we been sold as male and female slaves, I would have held my tongue, although the enemy could never compensate for the king's loss'" (Esther 7:3-4).

The king was horrified. He had no knowledge of an enemy who wanted to destroy his queen and her people. Of course, he didn't know at that point that Esther was Jewish, so he didn't connect her to the decree that Haman had sent out. He demanded to know who the enemy was. "Who is he, and where is he, who would dare presume in his heart to do such a thing?" (Esther 7:5).

Esther pointed at Haman. "The adversary and enemy is this wicked Haman!" (Esther 7:6).

Now it was Haman's turn to be horrified. He stood there in terror as the king stormed out of the room and into the palace gardens. He realized that his life was on the line and began to beg Esther to save him. In his pleading, he fell across the couch where Esther was lying—just as the king walked back in.

To the king, it looked like Haman was trying to molest Esther. Now his fury was uncontainable. One of his servants told him about the gallows that Haman had constructed to hang Mordecai and the king ordered Haman to be hung from it instead.

In the aftermath of the execution, Esther pleaded with the king to reverse the decree that Haman had sent out. He brought Mordecai in, gave him the signet ring and told him to send out a new decree.

It created an interesting situation. The original decree that gave authority for anyone in the kingdom to attack the Jews on the thirteenth day of the month of Adar could not legally be revoked, according to Persian law. Even with Haman dead, the king could not change it.

What Mordecai did was issue a decree that gave the Jews permission to defend themselves and to annihilate anyone who attacked them. When the day came, the Jews were ready, and overcame anyone who dared to try. As a result of that incident, the Persians developed a great fear of the Jews. Many even converted to Judaism.

Mordecai was elevated to the position that Haman had occupied and was given great wealth and authority. He was greatly honored from that day on.

A proclaimed fast brings in the miraculous. It gives you courage. It changes impossible circumstances in your favor. It overcomes prejudice against you.

How many times have you wished that you had greater favor on your job or in business? Fasting and prayer may be exactly what you need to do.

Mordecai found himself in favor, and he won promotion because of it. Mordecai was not alone, however. The book of Daniel begins with an account of Daniel and his friends going on a limited fast. They refused to eat the choice foods of the king. As a result, they found favor with those over them. "Now God had brought Daniel into the favor and goodwill of the chief of the eunuchs" (Daniel 1:9). This favor continued in Daniel's life, and he was steadily promoted until he became one of the most powerful men in the empire.

Another man who fasted and prayed to gain favor was Nehemiah. During the exile in Babylon, he heard of the plight of the Jews living in Israel and he determined to ask the king for permission to return to Jerusalem and rebuild the walls of the city. Before he approached the king, however, he prayed and he fasted (Nehemiah 1:4). He specifically asked for favor.

"O Lord, let your ear be attentive to the prayer of this your servant and to the prayer of your servants who delight in revering your name. Give your servant success today by granting him favor in the presence of this man."

"I was the cupbearer to the king" (Nehemiah 1:11 NIV).

Fasting and prayer resulted in Nehemiah being promoted from cupbearer to ruler of Israel. The favor of God moved him into a prominent position where he could accomplish great good for his people.

God promises favor to His people, which in turn, brings increase and promotion. "For You are the glory of their strength, And in Your favor our horn is exalted" (Psalm 89:17).

If you don't seem to be experiencing the favor of God, it is not because He doesn't want you to. His desire is to promote you, to exalt your horn. It is when we walk in faith that we are able to please God (Hebrews 11:6), and it is when we please God by walking in faith that we experience the full benefits of His favor. In order to live in faith, it might be that you simply need to spend some time fasting and praying so that your faith is purified. That is what Esther and Mordecai did. It's what Daniel did and it's what Nehemiah did. You can, too.

Summary

1. The story of Esther illustrates the importance of fasting not only for your own needs, but for others, including the nation.
2. Esther faced a crisis that required action. A man named Haman hated all Jews, especially Esther's uncle named Mordecai. Haman plotted to have all Jews in the kingdom killed.
3. Esther could do something that might result in losing her own life, but if she didn't do it, it would cost the lives of all her people throughout the kingdom.
4. Esther didn't just act, however. She proclaimed a three-day fast first. She gained several benefits from the fast.
   a. Fasting and prayer gave her favor with the king. Rather than have her killed when she came unannounced, the king granted her anything she wanted.
   b. Fasting and prayer gave Esther wisdom. Rather than presenting her petition immediately, she invited the king and Haman to dinner so that she could expose Haman in the most advantageous setting.
   c. Fasting and prayer gave Esther courage to face her enemy directly.
   d. Fasting and prayer changed what was certain death for Mordecai into increase and promotion.

e. Fasting and prayer brought deliverance for all the Jews in the country.

Application

1. At this point, you are almost ready to begin fasting. In your journal, take time to list areas that you can pray for that involve other people. This list might include friends or family that you know are going through a crisis. It could include the nation and our leaders as they deal with problems of the economy or terrorism. For this list, focus on others rather than yourself and your needs. Add these things to the purpose of your fast.

2. Continue your daily Confessions.

13

Preparing Yourself for a Fast

*I*n this chapter, I want to give you some guidelines so that you can get the greatest spiritual benefit out of a fast. We have seen how often people in the Bible fasted and what miraculous results they experienced. They approached fasting with prayer with certain disciplines and expectations and we should do the same. Done right, fasting will completely change your life.

If you haven't fasted before, don't try to do too much all at once. Take it slow. Start with one day or even one meal and work up to longer fasts. You need to condition your body to fasting, but you also need to prepare yourself emotionally and psychologically.

Proclaim Your Purpose

When you decide to go on a fast, proclaim your purpose. Set a date and determine exactly what you intend to accomplish.

What do you need God to do in your life? How long do you intend to fast? If you leave it open-ended, you will be much more likely to stop too soon. Decide ahead of time.

It is always a good idea to write down your goals. It helps you to be focused on them. Before you start a fast, get a journal and start writing down exactly what you are fasting about. Empty your heart of everything in your life that you believe needs to change, all the things that aren't right.

You might end up with several pages of things that you are believing God to deal with as you fast. It is all right to list them all. They are going to change as you move into pure faith. With mustard-seed faith, you will be able to pull out of eternity what is already yours in the Kingdom of God. Empty your heart by writing down everything.

Believe You Have Received

When you have finished writing out your list, believe that you have received your reward. Call those things that are not as though they are. Jesus said in Mark 11:24 that "whatever things you ask when you pray, believe that you receive them, and you will have them." The time to begin believing is now. Believe that you have received everything that you wrote down in your journal and you will have them. You are holding each one of those things up to God and receiving the promise for them. As you receive each one, write in your journal, "Done. I have it now."

This is an exercise of faith. When you pray according to God's will, that is, according to His Word, the Bible says that you will have the thing you ask for. "Now this is the confidence that we have in Him, that if we ask anything according to His will, He hears us. And if we know that He hears us, whatever we ask, we know that we have the petitions that we have asked of Him" (1 John 5:14-15).

Before you even start your fast, determine that you have already received what you are fasting for.

Go About Your Business

Jesus told His disciples how they should act when they were fasting. It was a common practice in Old Testament times to take on the appearance of fasting. People would tear their clothing. They wouldn't take a bath. They left their hair uncombed. They didn't brush their teeth. They sat in ashes and mourned. It was obvious when they were fasting. Everybody knew.

In Jesus' time, the Pharisees were known for the ostentatious way that they did everything. They wanted people to know that they were fasting, so they did all of the things that would draw attention to themselves.

Jesus told His disciples that He had a new way of doing things. Fasting wasn't about putting on a show. "But you, when you fast, anoint your head and wash your face, so that you do not appear to men to be fasting, but to your Father who is in the secret place; and your Father who sees in secret will reward you openly" (Matthew 6:17-18).

The disciples, when they were fasting, continued to do their work. Jesus said that we should do the same thing. We should wash and comb our hair, shower and dress well. We are to go about our business the same way that we normally would.

You may remember when we looked at the church in Antioch. Acts told us that while they were fasting and praying, they ministered. That meant that they were doing acts of love. They performed service. They were busy doing the work of the Lord. They worked and did good for others.

Your fasting and prayer is not a time for you to become selfish and focus all the attention on you and how much you are suffering without food. It is not a time for you to look for sympathy or approval from others for how spiritual you are. Instead you need to do your work, continue to love others and do good for them. Let the prayer and fasting be directed toward God and the cleansing that He is doing in you. Don't waste your time seeking attention from others. That won't accomplish anything of benefit.

Commit the Fast to the Lord

It is important to remember that the purpose of your fasting and prayer is ultimately to do the will of God in your life. With that in mind, commit your fasting and prayer to Him. The Bible does tell us to present our bodies to God. "I beseech you therefore, brethren, by the mercies of God, that you present your bodies a living sacrifice, holy, acceptable to God, which is your reasonable service" (Romans 12:1).

Prayer and fasting is a way of committing your body to God. Your body is the temple of the Holy Spirit. If your body doesn't work right, how can you fulfill your destiny? When you fast, you are saying to God, "I am doing this as a sacrifice to You. I want my body to be holy and acceptable to You." As you rid your body of pollution and toxins, you cleanse the temple so that it will work better. You will have more energy. You will be healthier. You will be a cleansed vessel, just as Paul described in 2 Timothy 2:20-21: "But in a great house there are not only vessels of gold and silver, but also of wood and clay, some for honor and some for dishonor. Therefore if anyone cleanses himself from the latter, he will be a vessel for honor, sanctified and useful for the Master, prepared for every good work."

When you fast and pray, you are cleansing the house where the Holy Spirit lives. You are sanctifying it by getting rid of the toxins in your physical system and the garbage of doubt and unbelief in your soul. You are cleaning out generational curses and things that hold you back, things that are not allowing you to do what God has called you to do. You are making yourself fit for the Master's use. You are getting rid of sin.

"Therefore we also, since we are surrounded by so great a cloud of witnesses, let us lay aside every weight, and the sin which so easily ensnares us, and let us run with endurance the race that is set before us" (Hebrews 12:1).

In prayer and fasting, we humble ourselves for the purpose of service, knowing that God gives grace to the humble. We are saying that we need God in our lives. We need Him to do a work in us so that we can make a mark on this earth. We can do something with our lives that will have an impact in building the Kingdom of God. The humbling that comes with prayer and fasting is important if we want our lives and our prayers to change the world.

"If My people who are called by My name will humble themselves, and pray and seek My face, and turn from their wicked ways, then I will hear from heaven, and will forgive their sin and heal their land" (2 Chronicles 7: 14). Commit your prayer and fasting to God as you humble yourself before Him and then your fast will bring in the miraculous so that you can see your world healed and changed.

Have an Attitude of Thankfulness and Gratefulness

Many times, people approach prayer and fasting with much complaining. We all like to eat and doing without food is not necessarily fun. When you feel that way, however, you are not acknowledging the good that comes from a fast.

Your attitude needs to be one of thankfulness and gratefulness. You need to be positive in what you think and what you say. You should be excited about the fasting and prayer and the cleansing that is taking place. You are changing spiritually. You are taking new territory and gaining victory. Don't be glum. Get excited.

"Let the word of Christ dwell in you richly in all wisdom, teaching and admonishing one another in psalms and hymns and spiritual songs, singing with grace in your hearts to the Lord" (Colossians 3:16). Psalm 100:4 says to enter His gates with thanksgiving and His courts with praise. We are to be thankful to Him at all times, blessing His name.

Have Self-Awareness

I had someone come to me one day with a question about prayer and fasting. She said, "Every time I go on a fast, as soon as I come off of it, I feel so depressed. Why do I feel so depressed after a fast?"

I told her that she felt depression because there was depression in her life, or possibly a generational depression. It was holding her back and the prayer and fasting enabled her to identify it.

Prayer and fasting will expose you to the spiritual world, both good and evil. Your physical body is detoxifying itself and as it does, you become aware of the toxins. You feel weakness and headaches and physical discomfort. You feel the effects of the poisons in your body being dumped into your blood stream. The same thing happens in the spiritual. Your soul detoxifies itself. Things that are contrary to the Word of God will come out of hiding and you will see them.

If you have rejection in your life, it will come up. You will suddenly find yourself feeling super-rejected. If you have a problem with feelings of worthlessness, it will become magnified. You will feel super-worthless. If you have a problem with perseverance, as soon as you start fasting and praying, you will want to completely give up more than ever. You will want to quit everything.

Whatever is a problem in your life will come up while you are fasting and praying. It will show its face. Do not panic and don't be surprised. There will be poison and you will feel the effects just as much as you do the physical poisons. But you need to get rid of them, so having them come to the surface is a good thing. Now you can deal with them.

You need to have self-awareness so that you can recognize the problems rather than give in to them. You don't want to embrace the garbage. You have to be able to step aside and take care of it.

This awareness of sin in your life is not the same thing as sin consciousness. When you don't know who you are in Christ, there is a tendency to identify with the sin instead of with Him. You think you are that sin. When you fast and pray and sin comes up, you identify with it. You embrace it. The devil hands you a whip and says, "Look at all that garbage in your life. You are no good. You are a rotten, terrible person." And you agree with him, so you take the whip and start to beat yourself up. That is sin consciousness.

Self-awareness, on the other hand, means that you know you have been made in the likeness and image of God. You know that the stuff coming up in you is not you. It is sin, but you don't identify with it. Instead, you identify with Christ. It is garbage that is in your house, but it is not the house. It just needs to go into the trash and be taken out of the house. The garbage is not you. It is what lives in you.

If sin consciousness is a problem for you, then you need to meditate on Romans 6. It says that you have been crucified with Christ. The old man is no more. He is dead and gone and you are a brand new creation. Then you can separate yourself from the sin that is in you. The Apostle Paul recognized the difference.

> "For what I am doing, I do not understand. For what I will to do, that I do not practice; but what I hate, that I do. If, then, I do what I will not to do, I agree with the law that it is good. But now, it is no longer I who do it, but sin that dwells in me. For I know that in me (that is, in my flesh) nothing good dwells; for to will is present with me, but how to perform what is good I do not find. For the good that I will to do, I do not do, but the evil I will not to do; that I practice. Now if I do what I will not to do, it is no longer I who do it, but sin that dwells in me" (Romans 7:15-20).

Paul was fully aware of the sin that was in his life, but he never identified with it. He knew that his identity was in Christ. He also knew that the sin needed to be dealt with just like trash. It needed to be taken out.

People often go to the other extreme. They don't identify with the sin at all. In fact they try to ignore it. They refuse to even look at all the garbage in their lives and the sin stays in them and keeps them from experiencing the blessings of God. You can't just leave it there. You must not identify with it and you must not ignore it. You need to see it for what it is and deal with it.

We set the sin aside, as Hebrews 12:1 told us. We take the time to clean house. That was the purpose for fasting, to cleanse. Don't be afraid of the sin. When you fast, it will come to the surface. That is good. Repent of it, and let the blood of Jesus cleanse it out of your life. You will be left with pure faith and that will move you into the blessings of God.

Control Your Environment

To succeed on your fast and not quit before you are finished, you need to be proactive about controlling your environment. There are several aspects of this to consider.

First of all, remember that you are going to be going about your day just as you normally would. Shower and wash your hair. Women, put on your makeup.

In most cases, you will be going to work or doing the things that you would normally do. Occasionally, you may want to get away so that you can focus completely on prayer, especially if it is a long fast. Some people like to get away to the mountains. Others prefer to stay at home. If you are able to do that, it will be of benefit, but for most people, that will not be possible very often.

Because you have to continue to function on your job, you want to consider how the prayer and fasting will affect you. If you have never fasted before and you are accustomed to eating a lot of junk food, you will find that your system is full of toxins and you will be much more likely to feel the effects, such as headaches and weakness. This will very likely make it difficult for you to keep up with your normal responsibilities, especially if your work involves a lot of physical activity.

Because you want to be able to do your work, you may want to start with a small fast, perhaps only a meal a day and work up to longer fasts as your system gets used to it. In the early church, it was common to fast from three o'clock in the afternoon until six o'clock the next morning.

Another thing you can do is start with a vegetable and fruit juice fast. That will clean the toxins out of your body slowly so that you can deal with it. You don't want to do something that will harm your body. Fasting is to bring you into health, so use some common sense. If you already have a healthy lifestyle, your system will be much better prepared for the effects of fasting and prayer and you will be able to do a little more. I have eaten very healthy for many years now and I don't have that much of a buildup in my body of things like chemicals and pesticides that so many foods have. As a result, I can now go on lengthy fasts and it doesn't impact my normal routine that much. Developing good eating habits is an important part of controlling your environment. It will make fasting and prayer much easier.

You can also proactively plan ahead. For example, you can prepare Scripture CDs or praise and worship music to listen to while you are fasting. Plant them in strategic places ahead of time. Put them in your car. Put them in the stereo in your house. Have them ready so that you can turn them on as soon as you walk in the door or as soon as you start the car. Plan time to pray and to listen to sermons, to Scripture and to worship.

Do not underestimate the importance of the Word of God as a part of your fast. The Bible refers to the cleansing power of the Word as similar to what water does. Ephesians 5:26 calls it the "washing of water by the word." Hebrews 10:22 speaks of "having our hearts sprinkled from an evil conscience and our bodies washed with pure water." The pure water is the Word. It cleanses your conscience and it washes away impurities.

This is an appropriate image. In fasting, your body is cleansed by water. The water you drink flushes the toxins out of your system. Toxins that come out through your skin are washed away by the cleansing action of a shower. Water cleanses.

The Word of God is the spiritual water that accomplishes the same cleansing of your faith. This is really the intent behind the description earlier in Hebrews of what the Word does. "For the word of God is living and powerful, and sharper than any two-edged sword, piercing even to the division of soul and spirit, and of joints and marrow, and is a discerner of the thoughts and intents of the heart" (Hebrews 4:12).

When we fill ourselves with the Word, it goes to work in us to bring the thoughts and intents of our hearts out into the open so that we can bring them into line with God's will and His purpose for us. The Word shows us what God says so that we can live in His promises. It is the Word that breaks every bondage in us and brings us life.

The problem is that sometimes our old habits and thought patterns are so deeply ingrained in us that we can't seem to get rid of them. Fasting and prayer enables us to cleanse the impurities out of our faith and connect to the Word. We must remember that fasting does not do anything for our faith by itself. It needs to be joined with prayer and we need to connect through prayer and fasting with the Word. It is that combination that is powerful. We don't twist God's arm and make Him do something when we fast. Rather, we connect to His Word so that it can change us. When we change, then things happen.

You need the Word to be a part of your fast. As you are cleansing your body, your soul will benefit from the washing of the water of the Word. Fill yourself with it. Saturate your mind with it. Confess it every chance you get. The power of life and death is in your tongue, so speak the Word. You will see miracles as you do. Speak the Word when you are praying. Speak it in the car while you are waiting at traffic lights. Speak it when you get up in the morning and speak it before you go to bed at night.

Summary

1. It is almost time to start your fast. To prepare, however, there are a few things that you need to do, so that your fast will be effective. These are the application of what you have learned.

Application

1. Proclaim your purpose and set a date to start. Decide how long the fast will be.
2. Write down what you want the fast to accomplish and believe that you have received what you are asking for.

3. Go about your business. Continue your work as normal. Don't dress or act in such a way that you call attention to the fact that you are fasting.

4. Commit your fast to the Lord. Humble yourself for the purpose of service and prayer.

5. Have an attitude of thankfulness and gratefulness. Stay positive.

6. Have self-awareness. The toxins in your life will come up when you fast. You might feel depression or rejection. If you are dealing with something in your life, it will probably become magnified. Recognize those things and separate yourself from them. Your identity is now in Christ.

7. Control your environment. Set aside time to be alone with God. Fill yourself with the Word.

14

The Fast with Prayer

*N*ow that you understand fully the benefits of fasting, it is time to actually go on a fast. Do not, however, just stop eating. There is a right way to fast and a wrong way. Done properly, a fast is very healthy. Done wrong, it can be harmful. Take time to do it right.

First, consult your doctor. There are some physical conditions that can be aggravated by fasting, and your doctor will be able to determine if you have any of those problems. It is a good idea, also, to make sure your doctor understands the benefits of fasting. Not all doctors believe in it. Find one who does.

There are times when you should not fast. Women who are pregnant or who are nursing should not fast. It will not be healthy for the child.

If you have certain illnesses, fasting can be dangerous if you are not monitored properly. A number of things happen inside you while you are fasting that puts considerable stress on your body. Blood sugar levels, for example, change drastically and that can be dangerous for a diabetic or if you are hypoglycemic or hyperglycemic.

The shock of all those toxins being dumped into your bloodstream can potentially affect your heart. If you have a heart condition, be sure that your doctor monitors the fast.

Since the liver and the kidneys are filtering organs, cleaning all of those toxins out of the blood puts extra strain on them. If you have liver or kidney problems, fasting can be dangerous. Be sure that your doctor supervises the fast in order to watch your reaction to it.

If you have any of these conditions, you definitely need to see your doctor before you begin a fast, and you should regularly visit him while on the fast in order to monitor your body's reaction. Especially when I go on a long fast, I make sure that a doctor checks my blood at least every couple of weeks, just to make sure there is no problem.

Water

The single most important thing to do when fasting is to drink plenty of water. That is not to say that you should go on a water-only fast. Because of the level of toxins and chemicals in our food and in the air we breathe today, a pure water fast would create too much stress on your system. It is best to go on a juice fast and allow your body to cleanse itself a little slower. It will be easier on your system. However, water is still the most important element, even in a juice fast.

Most people don't drink enough water normally, but when you fast, you especially need it. Without the water to cleanse your system, the toxins just build up. You absolutely need water. When Esther fasted, the Bible says that she did not eat or drink, but that was an extreme situation. Going without water for even a day can cause you serious harm.

You should double your water intake while on a fast. Plan to drink at least eight, eight-ounce glasses every day. The larger you are, the more you should drink.

You should only drink distilled water. You want it to be as pure as possible. You don't want any extra chemicals or pollutants. That's what you are trying to get rid of.

It is a good idea to put lemon juice in the water. Distilled water and bottled water have a slightly acidic pH balance, which enables it to be stored on the shelf longer. Lemon juice becomes alkaline in your blood stream and helps to neutralize acidic toxins. It aids the cleansing action of the water. Use fresh squeezed juice at a ratio of one lemon to a cup of warm water. Just squeeze it into the bottle and drink it.

I cannot stress enough how important water is. Drink lots of it. It is the best thing for you.

Before the Fast

The biggest mistake people make is to eat a big meal right before starting a fast and right after finishing the fast. I often hear people say, "I'm starting a fast tomorrow, so I'm having a big steak dinner tonight." A steak and all the things that go with it, like a baked potato, is one of the most difficult meals to digest that you can have. It will just sit there in your digestive track the whole time you are fasting and negate many of the benefits of the fast.

The preparation before the fast is as important as the fast itself, especially if you normally eat a lot of junk food and your system is filled with toxins. You need to ease into the fast by starting the detoxification process ahead of time.

It is best to lead up to the fast by eating only raw vegetables and fruits for at least two days before the fast begins. If you are going on a longer fast, you should probably start even earlier. Avoid sugar and salt. Stick completely to raw vegetables and fruit.

This preparation will start to get rid of toxins in your system so that you won't experience quite as much shock when you start a full fast. It will prepare your body so that fasting is that much easier.

The Juice Fast

There are different types of fasts that people use for health reasons. They are named for what you are allowed to eat. For example, a grapefruit fast means that you avoid eating any kind of food except grapefruit. When we talk about fasting for spiritual reasons, we mean doing without any solid foods. Because of the levels of toxins in most foods today, I recommend that you don't try a complete water fast, unless it is a short fast such as the 3:00 p.m. to 6:00 a.m. fast that the early church did so often.

Instead of a water only fast, you should do a juice fast. On a juice fast, you have no solid foods, but you do drink fruit and vegetable juices. You can also drink two cups of herbal tea each day. The juice fast is very healthy and will help you keep your energy levels up while fasting. You will still get the spiritual benefits of a complete fast.

Dilute all juices with water. Mix about one part water with three parts juice. Make sure that you use pure juices without any additives or sweeteners. The best juices for you are lemon juice or unfiltered apple juice. Grape juice is also very good. Avoid orange juice or tomato juice entirely.

It is a good idea to buy a juicer. You can find relatively inexpensive ones at your local department store. You can juice various vegetables and drink the juice as part of your fast. The best vegetables are beets, cabbage, broccoli, carrots and celery. Green drinks are those made from green leafy vegetables and they make excellent detoxifiers. When you juice raw cabbage, you should drink it right away. It loses vitamins very quickly after it is juiced.

As a general rule, you should not combine fruit juices with vegetable juices. The one exception is apple juice. It is good because it balances your blood sugar and it will give the vegetable juices a sweeter taste.

Apples juice is also a good starter in the morning. If you are used to starting your day with coffee or caffeine to get you going, apple juice will make a good substitute.

Speaking of coffee, don't drink it while you are fasting. Also, stay away from tea (except herbal tea) and soft drinks. Stick with fruit and vegetable juices and your fast will be beneficial to you.

The Three-Day Fast

If you have not fasted before, you should not try to do a forty-day fast right away. Start small and work up to it as your body gets used to fasting. In fact, as a beginner, you should probably start with just a day or even a meal or two.

Eventually you will want to work up to at least a three-day fast, however. Just for your health, it is good to fast for three days a month. It will keep your body relatively free of toxins and promote good health on a regular basis. Here is a simple plan for going on a three-day fast.

Before the fast, check with your doctor. Then, for two days, eat nothing but raw fruits and vegetables.

Day 1: Drink all the unfiltered apple juice that you want. Also, drink at least eight, eight-ounce glasses of water with lemon juice.

Day 2: Drink unfiltered apple juice diluted fifty percent with distilled water. Also drink eight, eight-ounce glasses of water with lemon juice.

Day 3: Squeeze the juice of eight lemons into a gallon of distilled water and drink it over the course of the day.

Day 4: Eat only raw fruit and salads. Drink eight, eight-ounce glasses of water with lemon juice.

Day 5: Eat normally.

The Longer Fast

It is good to go on a longer fast a couple of times each year. That can be anywhere from five days to twelve days. Most nutritionists recommend a three-day fast once a month and a ten-day fast twice a year.

For a longer fast, you can start the same way that you did with a three-day fast. On the fourth day, start drinking vegetable juices with apple juice each morning and each evening.

On the seventh or eighth day, you can start to add a whey protein shake or protein powder with water. You should also take vitamin supplements.

Breaking the Fast

How you break a fast is even more important than how you start it. Especially on a longer fast, if you do not come off the fast properly, you can cause yourself serious harm and potentially even death. Your digestive system has shut down and if you just dump a bunch of hard-to-digest food into it, your body won't be ready for it. The digestive juices aren't there and the bacteria in your system that help digestion have been cleaned out. The food will just sit there like a rock in your stomach.

I saw an example of how important properly coming off of a fast is when I was ministering in Russia. There was a pastor on the trip who went on a water-only fast for seven days. At the end of the seventh day, he broke the fast with a big steak dinner. He was lucky that he didn't die. It made him so violently ill for the next two days that he couldn't leave his hotel room.

As a general rule, you should take at least one day coming off of a fast for every three days that you were on it. If you fasted for three days, you need one day to come off the fast. If you fasted for ten days, take at least three or four days to come off of it.

Do not start out with anything greasy or difficult to digest. The best thing is to begin with a salad or fruit. Build up from fruits and vegetables to breads and grains and then to fish. Only then can you start to eat chicken and after that, red meat. You should wait as many days as you were on the fast before you eat protein. If it was a seven day fast, wait seven days before you have a steak. Let your system get ready for it. Start out with small portions of everything. Your stomach has been shrinking, so don't expect to put as much in it as you used to. Take your time. There is no hurry.

Do not come off of a fast with any kind of junk food. You don't need heavy fried foods. You also don't need potato chips or candy and cookies. Coming off on soft drinks can kill you. You just cleaned all of that stuff out of your body. Don't be in a rush to put it all back.

Enjoy Your Fast

For most people, the very idea of fasting makes them start to feel hungry. They absolutely hate fasting. Because they hate it so much, they avoid it and because they avoid it, they never experience the tremendous benefits that fasting brings.

It is possible to enjoy fasting. The way to do this is to recognize how much good it does for you. Once you have done it a time or two and you see how good you feel afterwards and you witness how powerfully God moves in your life when you are delivered from doubt and unbelief, fasting doesn't seem so bad. You can look at the benefits instead of the hunger and get really excited about it.

Fasting should be a regular part of your life, both for your physical health and for your spiritual benefit. As you learn to fast God's way, you will find yourself delivered of things you never thought you could get free of, you will see yourself healthier than you've ever been and you will see the miraculous turned loose in your life as never before. Fasting is a great tool to use in your life. Take advantage of it and enjoy the reward. Go into it with a great attitude.

Summary

1. The time has come. You are ready to begin fasting and praying. If you have not already done so, consult your doctor to make sure you do not have any physical conditions that would be aggravated by a fast.

Application

1. Drink at least twice as much water as normal. Add fresh squeezed lemon juice--one lemon per cup of warm water.
2. Begin a pre-fast diet by eating only raw vegetables and fruit for at least two days before the fast.

3. Do not fast on water only. Supplement the water with fruit and vegetable juices:
   a. Fruit juices:
      • Unfiltered apple juice
      • Lemon juice
      • Grape juice
   b. Juiced vegetables:
      • Beets
      • Cabbage
      • Broccoli
      • Carrots
      • Celery
4. Avoid orange and tomato juice.
5. If you have never fasted before, start small. Fast for one day or even just one meal. Work up to longer fasts. It is recommended that you do a three-day fast each month and a ten-day fast twice a year.
6. To break a fast:
   a. Do not fast longer than forty days.
   b. Take at least one day coming off the fast for every three days you were on the fast.
   c. Start with salads and fruit and work up to breads and grains, then to fish, then to chicken and beef. Wait as many days as you were on the fast before you start to eat protein again.

Fasting Confessions

I am keeping my body under control, making it subject to the Holy Spirit. (1 Corinthians 9:27)

During this fast, I am sanctifying, cleansing and detoxifying my body so I am fit for the Master's good work. (2 Timothy 2:20)

All my digestive organs are resting, and no toxins are being put into my body.

Fat and toxins are being broken down and expelled from my body.

My immune system is being strengthened through this fast. The aging process is being reversed in my body, and I am living a longer, healthier life.

My liver, kidneys and colon are being cleansed and my blood is being purified.

I am losing excess weight and water during this fast.

My breath and tongue are being cleansed.

My bones are being strengthened. (Isaiah 58)

I wholly commit this fast to You, Lord, presenting my body to You as a living sacrifice, holy, pleasing and acceptable to You. (Romans 12:1)

Fasting is a vital part of my Christian life.

I am humbling myself through this fast. (Hebrews 12: 1)

I am not gratifying the desires of the sinful nature. My flesh is under control.

I am seeing things in their proper perspective through this fast.

I am being cleansed from doubt and unbelief, and I have entered into mustard-seed faith.

Desires that are not of God are being resurrected back to what God wants for me physically and spiritually.

I am hearing clearly from God. (Acts 13)

My faith is purified. (Acts 13)

My faith and fasting bring supernatural increase and move mountains. (Acts 13)

God is rewarding me openly through this fast. (Matthew 5:16-18)

I am fasting as God has chosen. Bonds of wickedness are loosed off my life. I am completely free from oppression. Every yoke of bondage is broken off my life. Every heavy burden is lifted off of me through this fast. My light is breaking forth! My healing is springing forth speedily! My righteousness goes before me for I am established in righteousness. The glory of the Lord is my rear guard. When I call, the Lord hears and answers me. Through this fast, God is causing me to ride on the high places. (Isaiah 58:6-14)

I am abounding with the favor of You, Lord, and I am full of Your blessings. (Deuteronomy 33:23)

I win favor with everyone who sees me. (Esther 2: 15)

God causes all things to work together for my good. (Romans 8:28)

I am able to minister to others, bless others, and do the work of the Lord. (Acts 13:2, Matthew 6:17-18)

I am victorious over sin.

I am receiving direction and protection.

I have not been given a spirit of fear, but of power and love and a sound mind. (2 Timothy 1:7)

About the Author

Resolved to leave an imprint for this generation and generations to come, Dr. Maureen Anderson has been teaching the Word of God since 1976. She is counted among the most exciting and respected women in Christian ministry. Dr. Maureen exhorts everyone who will listen to confess God's word each day, which expands your "love walk" with Jesus. A best-selling author and international speaker, Dr. Maureen writes from her own experiences and shares how God's love, grace, healing and prayer has led her to live an extraordinary life. Titles include such favorites as *Confessing God's Word, Making Marriage a Love Story, Damaged DNA, Toxic Emotions, Making Impossibilities Possible* and recent favorite, *A Marriage Beyond the Dream*, born out of extensive research and over 45 years of marriage.

Dr. Maureen Anderson ministers alongside her husband, Dr. Tom, as Senior Pastors of The Living Word Bible Church located in Mesa, Arizona. Living Word is considered to be one of the fastest growing churches in the nation with over 12,000 in attendance. Also in full-time ministry with them are their two sons and daughters-in-law. Dr. Maureen also enjoys spending a great deal of time with her nine grandchildren.

Prayer of Salvation

God loves you—no matter who you are, no matter what your past. God loves you so much that He gave His one and only begotten Son for you. The Bible tells us that "...whoever believes in him shall not perish but have eternal life" (John 3:16 NIV). Jesus laid down His life and rose again so that we could spend eternity with Him in heaven and experience His absolute best on earth. If you would like to receive Jesus into your life, say the following prayer out loud and mean it from your heart.

Heavenly Father, I come to You admitting that I am a sinner. Right now, I choose to turn away from sin, and I ask You to cleanse me of all unrighteousness. I believe that Your Son, Jesus, died on the cross to take away my sins. I also believe that He rose again from the dead so that I might be forgiven of my sins and made righteous through faith in Him. I call upon the name of Jesus Christ to be the Savior and Lord of my life. Jesus, I choose to follow You and ask that You fill me with the power of the Holy Spirit. I declare that right now I am a child of God. I am free from sin and full of the right-eousness of God. I am saved in Jesus' name. Amen.

If you prayed this prayer to receive Jesus Christ as your Savior for the first time, please contact us on the Web at **www.harrisonhouse.com** to receive a free book.

Or you may write to us at

Harrison House • P.O. Box 35035 • Tulsa, Oklahoma 74153

Fast. Easy.
Convenient.

For the latest Harrison House product information and **author news, look** no further than your computer. All **the details on our** powerful, life-changing products are **just a click away.** New releases, E-mail subscriptions, **testimonies, monthly** specials—find it all in one place. **Visit** harrisonhouse.com today!

harrisonhouse

The Harrison House Vision

Proclaiming the truth and the power

Of the Gospel of Jesus Christ

With excellence;

Challenging Christians to

Live victoriously,

Grow spiritually,

Know God intimately.